Published by Investing for Good 2012

Copyright © Adrian Hornsby, 2012
All rights reserved

Investing for Good CIC
1 Regent's Place, London SE3 0LX, UK

www.investingforgood.co.uk

ISBN 978 0 9571603 3 0

THE GOOD ANALYST

Impact Measurement and Analysis in the Social-Purpose Universe

by Adrian Hornsby

FOREWORD

This book is about how a better understanding of social value can lead to a new set of relationships between society, money, and people's access to a healthy and fulfilling life. Money can be difficult to move around in society — getting stuck sometimes in the wrong places, or being imagined to be somewhere where it turns out later it's not (or not any more). In the social sector these difficulties are often compounded by money not really knowing where to go, or how to be effective. But there is a potential lead. As the sector is really about impact — meaning the social or environmental good that comes from doing something — by looking at impact, it is possible to send signals to money as to how to move. And so put more distinctly, this book is about how analysing social impact can inform and guide the flow of capital through the social-purpose universe to the places where it can do most good. As such, it is of immediate potential interest to:

- social-purpose organisations, such as **charities** and **social enterprises**
- providers of capital to the social sector, such as **funders**, **commissioners of social services**, and **foundations**, **funds** and **impact investors**
- experts within and around the sector, including **policy makers** and **advisers**, **regulators**, **consultants** to charities and donors, and **academics** and **impact researchers**

At the core of the book is a Methodology for Impact Analysis and Assessment (MIAA). The Methodology is aimed at looking at social-purpose organisations throughout the sector, and analysing their impacts in a robust and consistent fashion. To do this, it draws on measurements made at the ground level, and accordingly is accompanied by a set of Guidelines for How to Measure and Report Social Impact. These two documents form Parts II and III of the book, and make up the chief informational content.

PART II Methodology for Impact Analysis and Assessment (MIAA)
for reviewing the impact of social-purpose organisations

PART III Guidelines for How to Measure and Report Social Impact
for organisations looking to develop their own measurement systems

Part I provides an introduction to the approach, including an overview of how it all works, and a history of its development and use (see chapters 3 and 4). But any piece of analysis comes steeped in two kinds of information: firstly and most obviously, information relating to the object under analysis; but also, though often in more coded form, information about the person performing the analysis, and how they think. A methodology deflects some of this away from the individual analyst, but it rapidly falls back on the methodology itself, embedded within which will be the assumptions and opinions of whoever devised it.

To be transparent on this front, as no doubt our philosophy has shaped both the methodology and the results it produces, the introduction starts with an outline of where it has come from in terms of our ideas, our beliefs, and perhaps most importantly of all, our aspirations as to what it can do.

A good analyst, for the purposes of this book, is one who analyses social and environmental good, as well as one who does so well or skilfully, and is in this sense good at doing it. But there is a third meaning too, as like a good Samaritan or a good witch, a good analyst can I believe be a force for good, with a moral power and a social impact all their own. To grow impact and, as a society, to invest in it, we need to know where and how it is taking place. The purpose of a good methodology then is to speed the good analyst in the task of finding out.

Adrian Hornsby
Investing for Good, 2012

CONTENTS

PART I Introduction
1. Measure in Everything: A Brief History of Thinking About Impact — 11
2. Analysing Analysis — 23
3. The Investing for Good Methodology for Impact Analysis and Assessment (MIAA): Development and Overview — 40
4. On Using the MIAA — 69

PART II Methodology for Impact Analysis and Assessment (MIAA)
0. Prefatory Notes — 79
1. Mission Fulfilment — 81
2. Beneficiary Perspective — 114
3. Wider Impact — 133
4. Appendix A: Weighted Impact Scoresheet — 155
5. Appendix B: Impact of Contribution — 161
6. Appendix C: Beneficiary Perspective Indicator Tables — 169
7. Appendix D: Sample Diagrams — 218

PART III Guidelines for How to Measure and Report Social Impact
0. Prefatory Notes — 225
1. Defining Your Mission — 229
2. Mapping Your Activities and Measuring Your Impact — 234
3. Beneficiary Involvement — 245
4. Using Results — 250
5. Communication — 259

Glossary — 264
Further Resources — 267

PART I
INTRODUCTION

1. MEASURE IN EVERYTHING
A Brief History of Thinking About Impact

"If the Prince be too important, tell him there is measure in everything, and so dance out the answer."
— William Shakespeare, *Much Ado About Nothing*, II, i

The last decade has seen a meteoric rise of interest in the term "social impact measurement". From a place in third sector academia it has cut a path through think tanks and advisory bodies right up to the zeniths of government, assuming a prominent role in proposals as how to reform the ailing UK[1] — and, within development circles, the developing world. At the same time, social-purpose organisations have gasped and watched its ascent, wondering to some extent quite where it is going to land. For all that has been made of social impact measurement, no one yet seems to be entirely sure as to what exactly it is, how to do it, or what it looks like once it's done. And so, as with anything that both appears at large and fails to present a definitive form, questions have been raised as to its permanence and validity.

The principle, naturally, is much older than the blaze. Explicit work on social metrics dates back to the 1970s, when it also engendered interest among governments. The fundamental idea however has a much longer intellectual history, reaching back past Victorian notions of philanthropy to draw instead on a Renaissance humanist philosophy, and a conception of the universe as something fundamentally ordered, and thereby delightful to reason — a little like a divinely intricate clock, or a gorgeously structured piece of music. Within such a universe everything proceeds with measure, and can therefore be thought about in measurable parts. And it is precisely this that Shakespeare is playing on in *Much Ado About Nothing*, when the witty Beatrice remarks, "there is measure in everything", suggesting that the

---

1 Recent governments have expressed the intention to make welfare and social services provision more accountable, better evidenced, and more results-driven through the use of effective social impact measurement. The language of social impact runs throughout definitions of the Big Society and the ideas surrounding it. Big Society Capital, with its declared ambition to reshape the financing of the social sector, has vowed to be a "champion" of social impact measurement.

Prince "dance out the answer". Here "measure" is used to mean something knowable and precise, but also puns on a second meaning of measure as musical time — thus imagining everything in the world as a kind of melody, unfolding to its own particular rhythm, and amenable therefore to being measured out in bars, counted, and danced to.

Today equally a form of "dance-of-reason-thinking" underpins approaches to rationalising social phenomena. In the specific context of social impact measurement, it conceives of the work of social-purpose organisations as likewise adhering to an inner logic, which it then attempts to elicit, and understand structurally. The task of metrics is to look further to the components of this structure, and assign countable values. These two actions — the reasoning out of how an organisation does what it does, and the identification of ways in which to see that being done — form the basis for any kind of treatment of social impact. Accordingly all social impact measurement, reporting, analysis and assessment builds on a critical and explicit address of two things:

i. a description of the organisation's process
How is the social impact being achieved?

ii. an expression of the organisation's results
What are the kinds of social impacts being generated, and on what scale?

The aim of social impact measurement is not to replace more narrative-based approaches to the way social-purpose organisations tell their story. Rather it offers a powerful tool which, alongside individual stories, can help articulate the organisation's activities in a clear and transparent manner, and demonstrate the real effects these are having. The potential benefits of being able to do this are many, and felicitously are distributed in a win-win fashion across the various parties involved. These parties are worth drawing out individually as they are the key readers of social impact information, and it is their engagement — rather than that of governments, think tankers or academics — that ultimately will turn social impact measurement into a permanent and valid force in the social-purpose universe.

1. Social-Purpose Organisations
The primary users of social impact measurement are social-purpose organisations themselves. For an organisation to know with confidence which of its activities are proving successful, where there are improvements to be made, and how to optimise their operations with respect to social impact, some form of measurement is crucial.

Organisations that are capable of recognising their triumphs and failures are likely to be far more effective than those that aren't really sure what they are achieving. Indeed, an impact-driven or "for-impact" organisation that is not interested in measuring its impact would be as fundamentally nonsensical as a for-profit organisation that doesn't care to count its profits.

As this is increasingly being recognised, a lack of information around impact can in itself produce a negative impression of a social-purpose organisation. Conversely organisations that do engage with impact measurement automatically find themselves in possession of convincing evidence as to the benefits of what they do, and are thereby empowered to make a stronger case to donors, funders, commissioners and investors (a group henceforth referred to as capital providers). In the current context this implies a knock-on PR benefit to measurement, but over the longer term, and given the highly competitive market that exists for social sector funding, it may become critical to an organisation's ability to attract capital. Thus social impact measurement is likely to play a growing role not only in how organisations manage their impact, but also in how they survive financially.

2. Capital Providers
Equally for institutions or individuals driving money into the sector, the results of impact measurement feeding up from the organisations they support can form the basis for a better understanding of their own impact. This can in turn — just as with social-purpose organisations — lead to a better and more impact-sensitive management of funds.

The term "social return" is sometimes used to describe the concept of an awareness of social benefits flowing back to capital providers as a form of compensation, in lieu of or in addition to a financial return, for having put money in. On one level this is simply nice for capital providers, but more importantly, social returns can, like financial returns, play a critical informational role, providing signals to capital providers and guiding behaviour. Impact measurement is essential to ensuring that these social returns are evidenced in a tangible and meaningful way, and for them then to be effective in motivating and directing the sector.

3. The Social Sector At Large
The greater levels of transparency and understanding implied by impact measurement can further serve to galvanise the sector as a

whole. Better knowledge as to where and how money is being used successfully allows capital to follow impact, and for market-like efficiencies in its allocation.[2] This in turn supports a vibrant sector which is itself attractive to capital and likely to inspire growth. High levels of information exchange equally benefit social-purpose organisations, as it naturally leads them to be more aware of each other's activities, and thereby to share knowledge and techniques. This is likewise helpful for government as it allows government bodies to learn from the movements of an impact-led, or impact-measurement-led sector, and feed this intelligence into policy. At the same time advocacy groups, with a clearer picture of what the impacts in different parts of the sector are, are in a stronger position to make their case.

4. Beneficiaries and Staff

Ultimately the advantages of social impact measurement — through contributing to the development of better social-purpose organisations, better-informed capital providers, and a more dynamic and impact-driven sector — fall to the beneficiaries of the impacts themselves. This happens most obviously in the form of better-directed services and more services. However social impact measurement can also reach beneficiaries more immediately. Measuring and recording impact furnishes organisations with a means to communicate with beneficiaries about it, thereby supporting efforts variously: to improve awareness and expand outreach; to demonstrate what is achievable and help beneficiaries understand and chart their own progress; and, in the case of successful impacts, to recognise and celebrate change. This equally is of enormous value to staff working with beneficiaries, who through measuring impact in this way, are able to see the difference they have made. This unlocks possibly the most powerful motivational force in the sector as it goes to the very heart of why people engage with it in the first place.

---

2 This implies a market in which socially-motivated capital (grants, social investment) is administered on the basis of impact, with organisations that are able to demonstrate high impact performance accessing capital more easily and growing, and, necessarily, organisations with weaker impact performance finding it harder to access capital and failing. In such a context the presence of failure is actually an indication of a healthy sector, in that it shows that ideas that may or may not work are being tried (i.e. risks are being taken), and that capital is moving from less effective to more effective organisations. This does place a considerable burden of responsibility upon impact measurement, giving it in effect the power to make or break organisations. However if the measurements are good the net effects will be positive, as an informed market-place will easily outstrip a muddle.

Thus the advantages offered by social impact measurement are considerable and widespread. Indeed what becomes curious when looking at social impact measurement now is that it has taken so long for the sector to really start talking about it. If the benefits are in fact so great, why for example was this book not written decades ago?

The standard answer has always been that measuring social impact is simply too difficult. The "good" of any particular act is too intangible to be defined, and the different kinds of good that people engage with are too diverse, with edges too diffuse and outcomes too long term to be definitively counted or accounted for. This is contrasted with the commercial sector, where systems for financial measurement have long been established, but have only to deal with a simple bottom line. Against this, measuring good seems like an impossible task.

This traditional defence of the social sector, and its comparative paucity of measurement tools, starts to break down however when the practices of financial accounting are considered a little more closely. For in truth financial accounting faces a number of surprisingly similar problems. Many of the quantities going into a financial bottom line themselves represent highly intangible and diffuse-edged concepts, such as brand value, goodwill, intellectual property, virtual assets and so on. With regard to long term outcomes, bonds of all kinds and entire futures markets constitute explicit structures for talking about and making agreements concerning things that may or may not happen or be the case in ten years or more. Furthermore the entire discipline of measuring and managing risk, which effectively underpins all of finance, exists precisely because of the fact that there is a fundamental uncertainty at play (i.e. an asset seems to be worth one thing, but there is a risk that it may turn out to be worth something else altogether, or indeed nothing at all). Thus far from dealing only in simple things, the commercial sector has long been confronted by a panoply of values that are highly difficult to count or measure, and its response has been to develop a host of increasingly sophisticated techniques and instruments to crunch these into forms that are countable and tradable.

Indeed the sheer complexity of the financial instruments being used during the previous decade proved to be a major contributing factor to the financial crisis of 2008. And as a phenomenon the crisis demonstrated, if anything, the extent to which the things being priced and traded were beset by exactly the same qualities of intangibility, diffusion, uncertainty etc.. Most of all what was exposed was that not only are the very foundations of finance — i.e. the lending and investing of money based on measurements of risk — liable to sudden shifts, but moreover that the ownership and existence of money itself is, rather unnervingly, highly intangible, and potentially highly

disputable. For at the essential level, money is something that has meaning only so long as the people using it continue to agree about it, and to support the collective fiction of its existence. But it has no independent materiality, and unlike physical quantities such as matter or energy, there is no law of the preservation of money. As we have witnessed, money can in enormous quantities simply fold itself out of reality; and conversely, under different circumstances, people are equally able simply to call it into being. In neither case does the money go to or come from anywhere, and none of it is any more or less real than itself. There is nothing essential about money, and it follows that, for all the apparent "hardness" of the financial disciplines, there is nothing in the practice of financial measurement or accounting that is dealing with real or stable quantities.

This is not to suggest that, seeing as how both money and social impact are similarly intangible, diffuse and so on, equivalent structures should be set up in the social sector, including fiendishly complex collateralised impact obligations, social impact futures, impact derivatives, opportunities to short impact etc.. Rather it is to make that point that in differentiating social impact from money, it is easy to forget that money itself is nothing more than a social phenomenon. It is a convenient language for a particular kind of social value, and acts as a measure for that social value. But it is not ontologically different from other kinds of social value, such as social good.

In fact the disparity in measurement systems between the commercial and social sectors probably has much less to do with the immediate difficulties of measurement (both social good and money are extremely difficult to measure), and more to do with the history of measurement demand.

On the commercial side, the development of modern financial accounting was chiefly driven by the formation of stock markets. Essentially companies found that in order to raise capital from investors on markets — which was highly attractive in terms of the potential for growth — they had first to be able to give a transparent financial account of themselves. And to do this they had collectively to engineer techniques for measuring company value — in all its different forms, and in a way that could be regarded as consistent and representative across the trading market. What the stock market-investment model also implied was that, as a result of investors' ongoing concern in investee companies, and in particular of their desire to be able to keep trading company stocks, the companies were further required to supply an ongoing transparent account of their financial condition. These twin demands for up front and continuing information — both of them coming from the investment or "buy-side" of the equation — were critical to the establishment of a system of quarterly and annual financial reports, and all the financial measurement tools that underpin them.

In contrast, in the social sector there has been no such history. Far from following the stock market-investor model, capital inputs into social-purpose organisations have traditionally been packaged as donations. For the capital providers (i.e. those on the "buy-side"), this form has implied little or no necessary structural interest in the social performance of recipient organisations — either at the time the donation is being made, or ongoing over the period during which it is used to fund activities. This is not to suggest donors haven't been interested per se, but that the nature of their interest has not created a distinct demand for regular transparent "social accounting". The immediate corollary of this is that organisations themselves, in order to attract capital, have not felt the need to produce such figures, and accordingly the development of a set of standardised techniques for measuring and reporting social impact has not had anything like the same resources or energy devoted to it as its financial counterpart.

Historically the effects of this lack of social accounting have been compounded with a further structural peculiarity of the sector, which is that traditionally donation-like inputs have covered not only growth capital but also operating income. Again the contrast with the commercial sector is striking. With a standard for-profit company, aside from any investment coming in, income is generated via business operations within a primary market of customers. By this the income itself, and information about it captured by financial accounting, monitors success within that market, and thereby acts as an (imperfect) "listening device" or proxy-measure for the value of the company's products or services to their intended users. In the social sector however, the users of an organisation's social products or services (i.e. its beneficiaries) are often not themselves generating revenue, and therefore their sense of the social value being delivered is not directly represented within income figures. In effect, the listening device normally offered by financial accounting is not tuned to the organisation's social-purpose operations.

Ultimately this has left the social sector firstly without accounting practices that measure social impact directly, and secondly with financial accounting practices that are of limited relevance to its core social activities. The result is a confusing space in which, in order to exist, a social-purpose organisation is still reliant on financial factors (its ongoing operational viability and its capacity to attract in new capital and grow), and yet these are only weakly bonded to the social outcomes that are the organisation's true purpose and very reason to exist. Organisations may expand or contract without this reflecting the success or failure of their activities, and capital flowing into and throughout the sector doesn't known how to connect with what should be the driving concept of social good.

This hazy decoupling of finance and impact helps explain two commonly noted features of the social-purpose universe. First is that there is a "no Google" effect — meaning that it is very unusual for a social-purpose organisation to move rapidly from being a start up to running major global operations propelled by the rocketing growth of its own products or services. Second is that there are very few mergers between social-purpose organisations, even though many work in similar spaces. No doubt these are both in part features of a far less aggressive and appetitive culture than that which exists within the commercial sector. However they are also indicative of a context in which resources are unclear as to where to go. To be able to generate the kinds of revenues and investment required to become a sudden Google in a new space, or to outgrow and buy up competitors in an existing space, an organisation would need to be able to deliver strong signals to capital regarding the principles on which it moves. However in a sector where capital is socially-motivated, but without explicit metrics tracking social outcomes, and without market systems indicating where these outcomes are taking place, the signals are largely unavailable, and organisations and capital providers alike struggle in a vortex of incomplete information as to who is outperforming whom.

The situation is however changing. On one side there is a top-down drive from major foundations, government and relevant bodies to "professionalise" the sector. This involves necessarily establishing a more concrete relationship between money in and services out. It implies also an inevitable rise in the use of consultants, who bring with them an invariable enthusiasm for the invention and application of metrics. On the other side, and much more profound, is a general bottom-up surge in demand for organisations — social-purpose and commercial alike — to say more about what they are doing and the impacts they are having. This goes well beyond the social sector, and is part of a major contemporary sea change in our understanding of information, and our relationship with its collection, measurement, and distribution. The invention of the internet — almost certainly the most significant development in this regard since the invention of the printing press — has driven the change, massively increasing our general thirst for information, and our expectations around its worldwide accessibility. At the same time that information has become more global, globalisation itself, and our growing awareness of it, has led to a heightened sense of how interconnected much of this information is, and therefore has foregrounded the importance of it being collected and made publicly available.[3] The combination of these top-down and bottom-up pressures

---

3 The Freedom of Information Act (introduced in the UK in 2000), wikileaks, indymedia, the

has ensured that the trend of the past decade and a half has been toward institutions, users and an interested public alike all wanting to know more about everything. Specifically within the social sector, this has started to generate the kind of demand that was previously lacking for organisations to report upon themselves in a more complete and compelling fashion. And so the need for the tools to be able to do so, and thus the meteoric rise of social impact measurement.

The presence of this invigorated interest in the activities and outcomes of social-purpose organisations is readily observable on a number of fronts. Most obviously, almost all organisations now maintain a website, with the implied need for a clear description of what the organisation believes and does (through links such as "mission", "about us", "what we do" etc.), as well as frequent updates on current projects and notable achievements. Websites make it very easy for organisations to publish regular information about their social impact, and knowing that, for a high proportion of people interested in their work, this will be among the first things they see, the reasons and motives for preparing such information become considerably sharper.

In tandem, there has been a significant rise among grant-makers and commissioners in the social sector of contractual or contract-style arrangements. This signals a major shift away from a standard donor structure, and toward something closer to a purchaser one, in which the party providing the capital is in effect "buying" social outcomes, or at least the products or services they believe will lead to them. The move has ushered in competitive bidding processes and grants or services agreements with conditions, which require organisations to outline in advance their activities and anticipated social outcomes, and "purchasers" subsequently to follow up and witness their delivery. A system for impact measurement is key to both processes, and instrumental for validating the approach and ensuring contracts are honoured.[4]

---

blogosphere, social media, the growth in the publication of information through Corporate Social Responsibility initiatives and the Global Reporting Initiative, and many others, can all be seen in the context of this wider cultural shift. Note these phenomena spring from all sides of society, including institutions, private corporations, and grass-roots activism. Environmental issues have played a prominent role, creating a paradigm for individual engagement with global concerns through a relationship with information. Familiarity with this concept has fuelled its application in many other areas, which now encompass such wildly divergent issues as geopolitics, consumer practices, human rights, labour rights, ownership of the media, privacy issues, local communities, and the business of sharing of "likes" with anything from one to one hundred million "friends".

4 A large body of social-purpose organisations derive a substantial part of their income from acting as suppliers of social services to local authorities. Overwhelmingly these relationships are governed by contracts which include some form of impact measurement (e.g. the number

A further form of demand for impact measurement is starting to enter the social sector through the concept of impact investment. An impact investment is one in which a social-purpose organisation takes on investment capital to grow its activities, thereby furthering its social impact, with the plan to repay that capital, plus (where possible) a financial return alongside the social return. Repayment comes from the organisation's income, which may be made up of trading income from social activities or services provided, donorship income, revenues from a commercial division within the organisation (e.g. charity shops), or any combination of these. But for the socially-motivated or impact investor, alongside repayment concerns and the need to be assured of the financial side of the investment, is a necessary interest in the social outcomes of the organisation. Indeed the fact that the overwhelming majority of impact investments offer sub-market rates of financial return underlines the need for the social return to carry real meaning, and offer real value. To be able to do so, and so to guide investment decision-making and lead capital toward truly superior overall returns, the social return will need to be substantiated by trusted forms of social impact measurement.

The promise of all these developments is that, by creating a distinct demand for social impact measurement — which historically has been lacking — the social sector will now in its presence respond with the tools and systems needed to do it.[5] As with any form of measurement, a degree of standardisation will be required, including agreement over what one "measure" is, and consistency in terms of how it is applied. In particular the measure will need to be able to travel across the social-purpose universe, keeping its shape from place to place, and from one group of users to the next. This calls forth the idea of a kind of goodstick — something like a yardstick, but one that can be used to count up social good. A goodstick

---

of services supplied) and a case for the impact's social value. The recent development of Social Impact Bonds (first bond launched in September 2010 with further bond issues under negotiation) takes the model a step further, whereby investors provide the capital for social-purpose activities, and local authorities then buy the social outcomes upon delivery according to a pre-existing contract.

5 Already this is starting to happen, with increasing collaboration taking place between active parties, who find themselves in need of tools, and academics who are developing them. Notably major development institutions, such as the World Bank, which traditionally have been keen on techniques like econometric analysis, are expressing a growing interest in how similar methods can help determine whether or not they are achieving their social objectives. In parallel a new generation of funds and foundations, that combine business backgrounds with social missions, are looking for ways to apply aspects of business-skills to social and environmental problems. Both are working with academics and groups with ties to academic institutions, whose research on the more empirical aspects of impact has been geared explicitly toward informing programme-funding and policy-making.

would serve twin purposes: one, to set out the measurements necessary for the formation of a dynamic and information-rich market of social products, services and investments; and two, to beat lagging impact investors and social-purpose organisations to that market.

Impact measurement is about indicating where social outcomes are forthcoming, and what the scale of their impact is. By ensuring that information about impact is legible and compatible, it is capable of driving capital into the sector, and directing its flow. While in the past a deficiency of measurement has allowed capital and social outcomes to meander and miss each other, the current drive toward measurement offers a means to couple the use of money — which can best be seen as one particular form of social value — with a wider a fuller sense of social good.

2. ANALYSING ANALYSIS

The response to so much new demand — from the public, from funders and from impact investors alike — for more rigorous and better defined forms of impact measurement has, predictably perhaps, been new rounds of confusion. On the capital side, commissioners and grant-makers have wanted more information, but without a standard format to work with, they have laid out often uncoordinated and occasionally conflicting ideas about what they expect this to look like. On the other side, social-purpose organisations have been obliged to spend more time fulfilling different requirements around separate pieces of incoming capital, each with its own particular restrictions, and with no one willing to fund the not inexpensive processes thrown up by applying for and winning funding. At the centre, a notable absence of agreed terminology further complicates affairs, with certain common ideas going by multiple names and needing translation back and forth, while every now and then a seemingly broad term gets affixed to a very particular idea or piece of the space.

Alongside this, an impressive array of foundations, regulatory bodies and consultants[6] have turned their efforts toward the problem, drawing in also some support from the commercial sector.[7] The result has been a considerable burgeoning of initiatives, and a profusion of suggestions and competing systems as to how impact measurement should be done.[8] While this has indubitably contributed to the problem of non-standardisation, there are increasing efforts to come together. The energies of various conferences and networking events seem to be gravitating toward greater common

---

6 Notable organisations in this space include New Philanthropy Capital (NPC), New Economics Foundation (nef), Triangle Consulting, The Social Return on Investment Network (SROI), and the partnership of IRIS (Impact Reporting and Investment Standards) with GIIRS (Global Impact Investing Rating System) and B-Lab. Both the UK Charity Commission and the European Commission have likewise engaged with the question of impact reporting in the third sector. The Global Reporting Initiative (GRI), in alliance with the OECD and UNEP, has focused on how social and environmental reporting may be applied to the commercial sector.
7 Among others, PricewaterhouseCoopers, Deloitte and KPMG have all offered pro bono services to the development of social accounting. Mainstream banks such as Credit Suisse and Deutsche Bank, through partnership in the creation of microfinance funds, have brought their back office services and managerial skills to microfinance accounting. A variety of global corporations have lent in kind or financial support to non-profit organisations working on social impact measurement.
8 In 2011 the Foundation Centre's Tools and Resources for Assessing Social Impact (TRASI) directory listed over 150 tools and methods for looking at impact.

association,[9] with an implied sharing of knowledge, and a convergence of ideas and, perhaps in part, their formulations.

The advantage now of having had so many different parties working on similar problems is that a substantial area of common ground has already been beaten out. The considerable overlaps that exist among the various methods serve to corroborate certain core concepts, and through drawing these together it is possible to start assembling the elementary building blocks of a universal or standard model for understanding impact measurement.

THE STANDARD MODEL

Essential to almost any approach to looking at the impact of a social-purpose organisation is the initial elucidation of its impact chain. The impact chain is what connects the organisation to the generation of social benefit.

ORGANISATION → ACTIVITIES → OUTPUTS → OUTCOMES

Figure 2.1 the impact chain of a social-purpose organisation

By this, the organisation engages in operating activities, which result in direct outputs (e.g. services supplied, products distributed). As these outputs are absorbed into the lives of beneficiaries, they lead to outcomes, representing the actual social and environmental benefits achieved (i.e. the changes in people's lives and the environment resulting from the organisation's services or products). The sum of these outcomes forms the organisation's impact.

When first establishing an impact chain, it is important to ensure it is coherent — i.e. that one link in the chain follows the next with a strong sense of cause and effect — and reasonable — i.e. that the outcomes being claimed are indeed reasonably attributable to the links preceding them. The

---

9 2011 marked the launch of the Social Impact Analysis Association (SIAA), developed in partnership with Adessium Foundation, Bertelsmann Stiftung, New Philanthropy Capital and PricewaterhouseCoopers. It will operate as a membership organisation with the aim to share knowledge among social impact analysts and raise awareness of the practice.

chain sets out the scope and timeframe for the impacts that the organisation is primarily concerned with, as well as, where appropriate, acknowledging other factors that may be involved.

With a cogent impact chain in place, it is then possible to look to the individual elements within that chain with a mind to measurement. The outputs and outcomes, identified and separated out in the chain, are considered for ways in which they can be counted. This is done using indicators: legible variables that track the changes in quantity of the particular element being measured. By assigning indicators and monitoring them, it then becomes possible, via the established relationships within the chain, to follow the impact being generated.[10]

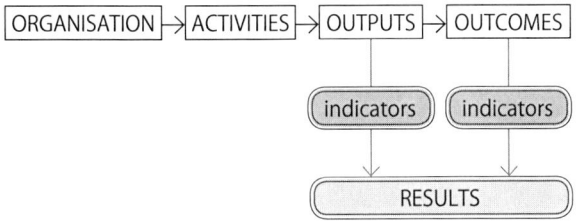

Figure 2.2 the impact chain with indicators being used to collect impact results

Behind the organisation is the capital provider, injecting the capital required for the organisation to be able to pursue its operating activities. The impact results rolling off at the other end of the chain go into an evaluation of impact performance, which feeds back to the organisation to inform strategy, and feeds up to the capital provider in the form of a social report, establishing the basis for the social return. At the same time, the operating activities are monitored by traditional forms of financial accounting, producing an operating income, and in the case of impact investments, a financial return. Adding these flows to the system produces the completed diagram (see Figure 2.3).

An impact chain with indicators monitoring the outcomes and outputs, and with the resulting information on impact being fed back to

---

10 A full treatment of impact chains, indicators and their defining qualities is given in the Guidelines for How to Measure and Report Social Impact (Part III) and in the Methodology for Impact Analysis and Assessment (Part II)

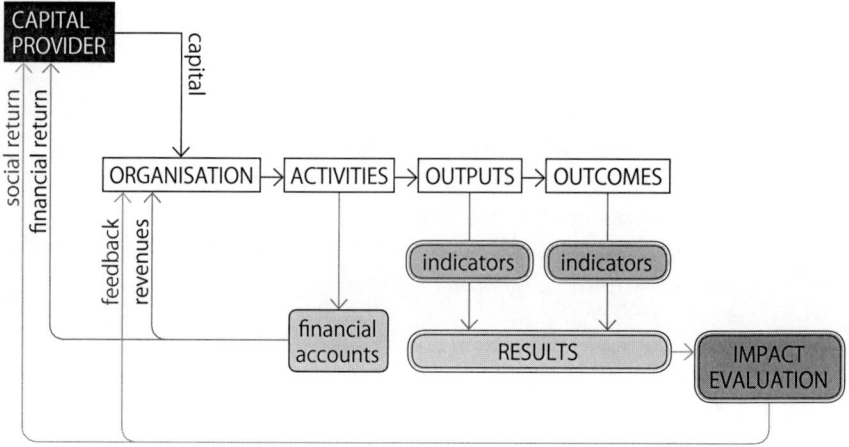

Figure 2.3 the full standard model

the organisation and the capital provider, forms the essential framework underpinning almost all approaches to impact measurement. It provides the standard model for how to understand the generation of impact by an organisation, and how to go about assessing how much of it is being generated.

In application across the social sector, this model implies two conditions which, stemming from the fundamentals of its structure, can therefore be seen to be systemic to social impact measurement itself.

1. Individual Generation
The first point to note is that impact chains are highly specific. They link a particular organisation's operating activities to its outcomes, and reflect these back to its own unique mission. Given the extremely heterogeneous nature of the social sector, within which substantial pride is taken in innovation of approach and singularity of vision, impact chains are not only multifarious, but fundamentally peculiar to individual organisations. The impact chain itself is a matter of individual generation by a single organisation as it maps its journey from mission to impact. This is true even for organisations working in similar fields and with similar operating models, as the chains of each

will be sensitive to the particular location of operations, the specific beneficiaries involved, and the organisation's own distinct aims.

2. Composite Discontinuity
Given that impact chains and therefore measurement frameworks are unique to individual organisations, it follows that the results produced are not readily compatible. The indicators being tracked are inevitably dissimilar from one organisation to the next, and while well chosen indicators will yield comparable year-on-year results for a single organisation, it is self-evident that organisations tracking different indicators are dealing with different quantities (for example, one organisation may track the number of microloans it has disbursed in Uganda; another the number of jobs created in the UK). As such, values in social accounting are not fungible, and though result-taking may be quantitative, the resulting quantities cannot logically be added, subtracted or submitted to direct comparison. Even organisations working with the same indicators will use different approaches, and do so in a way that will invalidate any one-for-one treatment of results (e.g. three employment-focused organisations may all count the number of jobs created in the UK, yet focused variously on homelessness, the long-term unemployed, and a specific deprived area, the numbers will not be like-for-like). Values in social impact measurement, and the kind of social accounting they directly support, may be coherent and continuous for the individual organisation, but a composite section of the social-purpose universe will exhibit discontinuous sets of accounts.

It follows from these two conditions of individual generation and composite discontinuity that social impact measurement is a practice whose primary level of application is that of the single organisation. The outputs, outcomes and overall impact of an organisation may be tracked and accounted for within the context of its own system, using its own iteration of the standard model, but there is no readily available currency for relating it to the impact of another organisation. And just as the measurement is applied at the level of the single organisation, the immediate relevance of the results will likewise be to the measuring organisation itself, and to those directly concerned with its success (e.g. its funders, investors).

This does not by any means invalidate the usefulness of social impact measurement. As noted earlier, social-purpose organisations and their capital providers are the two most obvious parties that stand to gain from engaging in impact measurement. The non-compatibility of results between

organisations does not compromise the power of measurement to indicate on an organisation-by-organisation basis: how effective an approach is proving; what difference any new strategies implemented might be having; and where there are improvements to be made. This knowledge remains crucial for effective management, which of course is likewise operating at the level of the single organisation.

The prospect however when looking out across multiple organisations is of an atomised universe of standard model measurement systems being applied to and used in unique and thoroughly specialised locations. And in accordance with this, groups looking to do work in the field of social impact measurement have tended to focus on these specialised locations, and on the individual organisations working within them. Foundations and consulting companies in the impact measurement sphere are for the most part social-purpose organisation-facing, typically seeking to offer their services to individual charities and social enterprises to help them establish their own specialised frameworks, and to develop these frameworks into full internal assessment vehicles with, where possible, a built-in reporting component.[11]

A plurality of individual measurement systems and reported results has ensued. However important forms of standardisation are nevertheless emerging. Notably, while each system may be individually generated, it is possible to look to the means of generation, and start laying out a procedure for how organisations build their impact measurement systems. An increasing recognition of the standard model lays the basal layer for this, helping organisations to think first about defining their impact chain, then selecting appropriate indicators, then integrating the monitoring of these indicators into working procedures, and so on.

In parallel with this evolution toward structural standards, much work has also been done on refining and collating sets of indicators. Indicators are by nature specific to particular fields of operation, and will never be

---

11   To give a few examples: NPC focuses on sector by sector work, but with the intention to make this work available to individual charities along with bespoke impact measurement advice services. Triangle Consulting likewise offers to work with charities to devise systems to measure the particular outputs and outcomes of their activities. The IRIS initiative has led to an online catalogue of indicators used in different sectors with the aim of making these available as a resource to individual organisations looking to develop their own reporting systems. In 2009 the SROI Network published with the Cabinet Office its guide "for people who want to measure and analyse the social, environmental and economic value being generated by their [own] activities". While SROI analysis does yield a number "score" (e.g. 14%), which would seem to have a more general sector-wide application, SROI practitioners stress that the SROI ratio is not to be treated comparatively, but rather is useful for the individual organisation to analyse the relationship between its cash inputs and its social outcomes. Again, the measurement is primarily for the measurers.

universally applicable across the social sector. However they can be shared by organisations working within those fields, and while the detailed application of indicators, and especially the interpretation of indicator-values, will remain organisation-specific, a common pool of indicators can be made available for organisations to draw on, or to use for guidance when creating their own.

These developments suggest a formalisation of two things: firstly, a set of guidelines on how to measure and report social impact — not a system for measurement, but a set of principles for developing a measurement system, along with advice as to how to go about it. And secondly, a dictionary of indicators — bringing together in one place the wealth of indicators currently in use (or suggested for use), along with some key information about them (e.g. what field they are used in, what outputs or outcomes they relate to, particular techniques for taking readings, and so on).

Both of these things, to a greater or lesser extent, exist already in various forms, and indeed this publication marks a further contribution. Part III is comprised of the Investing for Good Guidelines for How to Measure and Report Social Impact, and with it come links to the online Dictionary of Indicators.[12] Neither of these represent wholly original material or a massive departure from what is out there already. On the contrary, they draw considerably on the wide body of existing literature[13] and present an understanding of best practice. The Guidelines aim to provide a lucid walk-through of the key processes involved in creating a system that will be robust and meaningful for the organisation involved, and will accord with the predominating ideas across the sector. It is, we believe, both compatible with other established principles, and coherent in and of itself. The Dictionary we have made available as an online resource. It collects indicators gathered from a wide range of sources, streamlines them (i.e. knocks out doubles or near doubles), and groups them according to application. The Dictionary is best maintained as an online resource, subject to continuous revision and expansion as further developments are made in social impact measurement, and the population of indicators increases. We believe a powerful means to develop this resource would be to create an online Wikidictionary, which would allow organisations not only to access the resource, but also as they

---

12   For more on both of these see Part III, Guidelines for How to Measure and Report Social Impact.
13   Of this there is much, including publications from many of the organisations listed above. Notably in 2011 NPC, with the Cabinet Office, published a set of Principles of Good Impact Reporting. The SIAA has also suggested it will look to develop common principles among its members. The Foundation Centre's TRASI directory is the largest single online resource of toolkits, guidelines and principles. See the list of Further Resources at the back of this book.

modify and hone indicators through practice, to update and add to it. The best test of existing indicators, and the best field of innovation for new indicators, will necessarily be among the organisations using them, and so to ensure the Dictionary remains responsive and flexible to their needs and ideas, we believe it will be best served by an open rather than top-down content structure.

These two contributions — the Guidelines and the Dictionary — are chiefly a distillation of existing knowledge, and present a suggested conceptual architecture, as well as practical steps for implementing, common best practice. The development of a sector-wide understanding of best practice, and the emergence of standards that will accompany it, will make impact measurement and reporting simpler and thereby cheaper for organisations to undertake (as well as harder to avoid). It will also make the results more recognisable and more widely comprehensible for followers of impact.

What progress on this front will not do however is address the systemic issues thrown up by the standard model — i.e. those of individual generation and composite discontinuity. These needn't be a problem while acts of measurement stay focused on the individual organisation, and indeed both the Guidelines and the Dictionary remain firmly within these bounds, and the relatively well-established field of offering impact services to social-purpose organisations. What we wanted to do at Investing for Good however transgressed these bounds, and so required us to look beyond.

INVESTING FOR GOOD

Investing for Good is unusual within the social-purpose universe in that it was founded looking not toward social-purpose organisations, nor toward philanthropic foundations or philanthropists per se, but toward investors. Investing for Good is positioned to face the "buy side" of the investment market — including capital providers such as banks, asset managers and individual impact investors — and offer these parties advisory services over how to connect with socially-motivated financial products, and the social-purpose organisations and funds that underpin them.[14] On account of this somewhat singular business model we brought a distinct set of needs to the social sector — notably the need to look across the universe of different organisations in different specialised locations, and to compare

---

14 Investing for Good's services include investment advice to institutional and individual impact investors and guidance on portfolio management. We also work with social-purpose organisations on structuring financial products such as bonds for charities.

them explicitly with one another. Furthermore, the investment structures we were dealing with implied the kind of embedded ongoing interest in investee organisations that characterises financial sector relationships, and brings with it a corresponding level of expectation around measurement and reporting — both with respect to financial performance and social impact. To be able to meet this interest and provide clients with high quality advisory services ranging across the sector on the subject of impact required two things: firstly that the organisations offering investment propositions engaged with impact measurement and reporting themselves on some level; and secondly, it required us to engage with the resulting body of impact information, with all its systemic discontinuities, and to relate individual organisations within it to a sector-wide understanding.

This secondary engagement effectively creates a further layer of thinking about impact. It takes the primary layer of captured impact data, and reviews and analyses it. By laying this analysis over the reporting it is possible to absorb the disruptions within the primary data, and achieve interpretations that take place within a broader context. Our aim was still to look at individual organisations — and in particular at their investment offerings — but further to analyse them, and arrive at assessments that were specific to organisations, but that could stand alongside each other on a plane of meaningful consistency (see Figure 2.4).

For the consistency of the plane to be maintained however, it was imperative for the analysis itself to be consistent. If the organisations were going to be crunched one by one through analysis, it was necessary to have a means for performing that analysis in a way that would produce coherent results on a stable basis, and therefore we needed an explicit and formalised analytical process.

This in effect was the starting point for the contents of this book: a business need to develop a single methodology for analysing and assessing organisations operating across the social-purpose universe. The inputs to the methodology would be information gathered from and about the organisations themselves (using the organisation's social reports, general research and direct contact); the outputs would be a series of Investing for Good impact analysis reports — each one treating a single organisation and appraising its operations and impact, and together forming a continuous body of impact assessments. These assessments would support, for our purposes, advisory services to clients. But in a larger sense, we anticipated that the approach and the methodology itself would be applicable to any

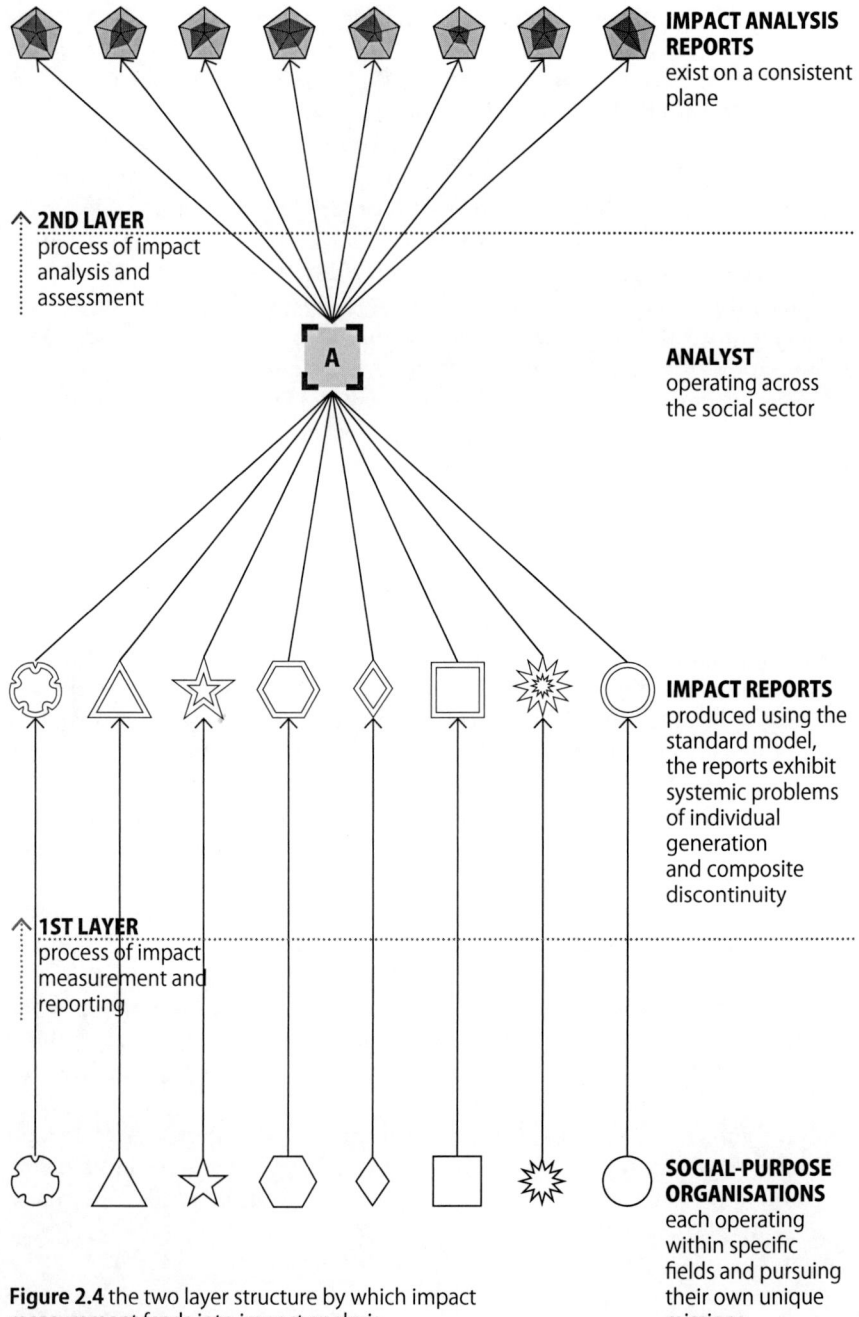

Figure 2.4 the two layer structure by which impact measurement feeds into impact analysis

THE GOOD ANALYST INTRODUCTION

situation where there was an interest in reviewing different impacts in a consistent fashion.[15]

The first thing to acknowledge when it comes to developing such a methodology is that it is neither feasible nor desirable to engineer a system that will produce results in a fully determined or mechanistic fashion. Because of the essential dissimilarity of the variables involved — the different outputs, outcomes, indicators and impacts — it is not possible to feed raw information from across the sector directly into a single automated process with no further application of human intelligence. As such, a methodology for impact analysis is unlike, for example, a coffee grinder, which requires only that beans be dropped in the top and someone crank the handle. Or to use a more contemporary example, it is equally unlike a computational analysis system, in which a fully composed set of algorithms manipulate the data entered and themselves produce the analytical conclusion. Crucially with both the grinder and the computational model, the person operating the system has no influence over the result, as they have in effect been engineered out of the process. This is not the case with impact analysis, which cannot be reduced to a formula, nor structured so rigidly as to efface the role of the analyst.

The continuing presence of the analyst, and the importance of their role, is a critical point for impact analysis, and one that goes to the core of how we as a society understand the treatment of information, and what analysis itself really is. It's a point that warrants a little further treatment as it very much sets up the relationship between the analyst and the methodology, with major implications for how to construct such a methodology, and how to regard it. It also touches on the considerable risks that analytical methodologies can throw up.

Historically analysis as a practice has had a curious development. In cartoon terms it breaks loosely into two panels (see Figure 2.5). Firstly, during the premodern era, analysis was dominated by essentially mystical relationships. A haruspex for example would study the entrails of a sacrificed animal, perform an analysis, and thereby produce an interpretation of the weather, or a medical case, or a prospective war etc.. By this the analytical result was wholly dependent on the relationship between the information (in this case the entrails) and the individual analyst (the haruspex), who therefore remained at the heart of the process.

---

15 For example, a financial intermediary or fund may wish to review the impact of its borrowers and investee organisations; a grant-maker or local authority commissioner may wish review the projects and organisations it funds; a social exchange or platform may wish to review the organisations it lists, and so on.

When presented in such terms it is easy to disregard this kind of analysis — and equally easy to forget that it held sway for most of the history of human civilisation, and indeed remains deceptively present today (though often in more sophisticated forms of dress). The social power of haruspices and haruspex-like analysts has been both remarkable and formidable. However their analytical power has been questionable, and their findings largely unreliable. This has left them vulnerable to a rival form of analysis, emerging as the scientific method, which has come to dominate the post-Enlightenment era, throwing up the second cartoon panel. Crucially a new relationship is created here: one that exists not between the information and the analyst, but between analysis and fundamental truth. What scientists discovered was that by observing physical processes, and analysing the resulting information, they were able to derive physical laws that existed and operated by themselves. Thus having discovered a law, it could be applied throughout the physical universe, independent of the original analyst and irrespective of who was applying it, and correct results would nevertheless be produced. A core strength of this was that the individual human element in the interpretation was removed. You could take the scientist away from the scientific principle and it would still hold. This is markedly different from taking the haruspex away, which just leaves you with a pile of entrails (see Figure 2.6).

Since its development, the scientific approach has proved so immensely powerful in application and predictive accuracy — in effect creating almost all the major physical characteristics of the modern environment — that it has inspired analysts in every other area of human thought to try to replicate some of its features. In particular efforts have focused on this aspect of removing the results of analysis from the people who arrive at them, with the aim of creating the same aura of depersonalised legitimacy. Very often the use of mathematics has been seen as key to this, and accordingly practitioners of different disciplines, in their respective pushes toward science-replication, have sought various means to generate numbers from their research in order then to be able to perform mathematical operations upon them (customarily accompanied by a form of discipline-specific "sciencese"). The flaw with this on the mathematical level however is that mathematics itself, however rigorously carried out, is only able to preserve truth. In essence mathematics takes an initial set of true statements, and works to rearrange the components and establish other relations that are also true. But what mathematics cannot do is reify an insubstantial starting point, and in applications within the social universe this problem is particularly acute as — unlike the mathematics used in the physical universe, which is grounded in fundamental physical truths — in social sciences and areas of social study,

Figure 2.5 the haruspex (top) relies on an essentially mystical relationship between the information and the analysis; the physicist (bottom) replaces this model with a relationship between analysis and fundamental truth

very often such truths do not exist. Social dynamics are subject to change, and so the mathematics used to describe them is liable to prove false all of a sudden, and with no necessary mathematical error.

The ironic upshot of this is that the application of science-like techniques to social fields has at times actually had a mystifying rather than demystifying effect. The presence of pieces of seemingly hard science has served to mask root uncertainties, and the subjective interpretations that have been performed around those uncertainties. At the cosmetic level the individual analyst is indeed engineered out, as per the scientific approach, by means of the design and use of analytical systems governed by mathematical operations. However, in the absence of a relationship with fundamental truths or concrete observations of universal physical behaviours, these operations inevitably lead back to the initial analyst who devised the system. The individual human element very much remains, almost like a haruspex in the machine, but has been hidden away behind mathematical or computational processes.

The use of replica-science to cover over what were in effect human ideas about how social systems operate was indubitably a significant contributing factor to the financial crisis of 2008. Financial products and strategies were engineered using mathematics that was itself underpinned by interpretative "takes" or "bets" on economic conditions. The impressive complexity of the engineering served to increase the impenetrability of the cover it provided, and the cover in turn had the effect of inspiring levels of confidence that were incongruous with the validity of the initial takes and bets. This confidence then distorted the very fabric of the economy on which the takes and bets were based, thereby rendering them false, and consequently falsifying also all the associated mathematics, and the products and strategies engineered out of it. This led to the challenging situation of financial institutions finding themselves operating in line with highly sophisticated analytical processes which proved to be simultaneously mathematically precise and in the real *social* world, deeply wrong.

When dealing with and analysing social quantities, such as money, risk or indeed social good, there is an impulse to devise processes that process out the analyst on the grounds that this makes them seem stronger and more objective. This apparent objectivity can however have a meretricious and ultimately destabilising effect. Worse still, it is bound ultimately to prove false, as it is based on a paradoxical effort to get rid of the human element when looking at aspects of reality that are themselves real only to humans (i.e. social systems, social values). As for the analytical power of such seemingly hard approaches, they often suffer when dealing with complex

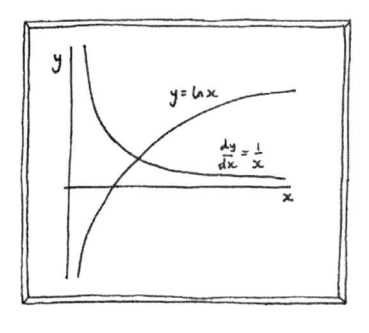

Figure 2.6 the removal of the physicist (bottom) has no bearing on the validity of the graph; the removal of the haruspex (top) leaves only a dead ram

social problems from not being able to incorporate the individual social intelligence of the analyst who is applying them.

In the specific context of the social-purpose sector, where the quantities being treated are necessarily discontinuous if not unique, the need for nuanced individual case by case analysis is even clearer. It is the individual analyst who is able to investigate the singular impacts of any organisation, and the analysis produced will be more robust for being sensitive to this understanding. This does not however imply a reversion to the complete subjectivity of the haruspex, nor does it dispense with the idea of process. What the concept of a methodology instead puts forward is a standardised means for performing individual acts of social impact analysis.

Confronted with different impacts reported from different contexts using different measures, the analyst is nevertheless able to look at things in a systematic fashion. The standard model and the emergence of established ideas around impact reporting best practice provide an immediate starting point. Using these, the analyst is able, in a reasoned and concrete way, to distinguish good reporting from poor — e.g. look for the presence of a cogent impact chain, verify the use of appropriate indicators to evidence outcomes, and so on. From here the analyst is then able to consider these evidenced outcomes, and explore the ways in which they have directly affected people's lives — e.g. see that the intended social benefits are indeed forthcoming, ensure that they are valued by beneficiaries, and so on. Further to this, the analyst can look to how they play into larger social change — e.g. observe the effect upon communities, review the relationship with other stakeholders and with the context itself, and so on. Each of these areas present specific phenomena that can be identified, investigated and appraised. Moreover a specific set of techniques for doing so can be drawn out and assembled into a formalised approach.

The Investing for Good Methodology for Impact Analysis and Assessment (MIAA) represents precisely such an approach. It is not a formula, but a clearly-defined analytical framework that allows for nuanced case sensitive interpretations, while ensuring the resulting assessments are arrived at through the application of a consistent and fully standardised procedure. It establishes a rationalised structure for the collection and synthesis of different kinds of quantitative data and qualitative information — both crucial for evaluating impact — and for relating these to a cross-sectoral understanding of social value. For the individual analyst looking at a single organisation it provides a toolkit, lining up questions and defining parameters. And for multiple analysts looking at different organisations, it supports a common and stable basis for making reasoned judgements. The resulting analysis places the organisations and their impacts on a single plane where they can be viewed, and considered for their key features, comparative impact performance, and overall attractiveness to capital. This allows institutions and individuals looking to inject money into the sector to integrate thinking about impact into their decision-making processes in a tangible, transparent and explicit fashion. In so doing, the methodology lays a foundation for the kind of coupling of capital with impact discussed in the previous chapter.

3. THE INVESTING FOR GOOD METHODOLOGY FOR IMPACT ANALYSIS AND ASSESSMENT (MIAA)

Development and Overview

Development

To recap very briefly: the Investing for Good MIAA was drawn up in response to a business need. In order to substantiate our advisory services, we wanted to be able to provide specialised reports on impact investments (i.e. investment opportunities in social-purpose organisations or funds). The concept for these reports was that they would take the primary reporting of the underlying investee organisation, supplement it with further research, and add a layer of analysis on top to produce an assessment, and ultimately a rating. These analyses and ratings, stemming from a position of cross-sectoral expertise, would play a critical role in defining Investing for Good's position in the market, and in informing our services to clients.

Building an analytical methodology was an iterative process. In 2007 we started writing reports and developing our ideas for a ratings system. Each time we finished a report we would send it back past the organisation concerned to confirm its accuracy, and to discuss the fairness of the analysis. These discussions, and a development-through-praxis approach, served to hone our analytical strategies, and shape the methodology itself. They proved instrumental on three main fronts.

- Firstly, through performing analyses and talking with investee organisations, we were able to see where our techniques were missing social value. The key challenge for a methodology, and especially in so a diverse space as the social sector, is to be able to recognise and capture all the different kinds of social benefits organisations are able to produce (indeed a methodology most obviously breaks down when confronted with an organisation that is clearly achieving significant social impacts, and yet these are not being acknowledged in the analysis). Social-purpose organisations would point out things we had failed to capture, and so lead us to incorporating them into our approach.

- Secondly, it is crucial that among things a methodology does capture, it does not attribute excessive value to one or another area so as to produce a bias or skew in the analysis. While feedback from social-purpose organisations would most often address underweighting, the process of doing multiple assessments across a broad field indicated places where minor elements were exerting an excess influence over results.

- Thirdly — and inevitably this was the most contentious part of discussions — we talked with social-purpose organisations about areas where we had been unfavourable in our analysis. Organisations engaging with social impact, and especially when trying to raise capital, are extremely keen to be reviewed positively. These exchanges forced us to be able to produce clear and convincing arguments for any negative assessments we had made. The result for us was the development of much more robust analytical techniques, and the carving out of tested and defensible positions within a space that traditionally has been exposed to very little critical assessment. It also, for social-purpose organisations, served to indicate areas of potential weakness in their impacts or impact reporting.

Drawing on this process, in 2008 we started to assemble our techniques into a formal structure, and in 2009 produced the first version of a fully orchestrated methodology. Since then over a dozen analysts have been trained in using the methodology, and over a hundred impact investments and their underlying social-purpose organisations have been processed through it. In addition to internal use, the methodology has supported our impact consultancy services to a number of funds and intermediaries who have wanted to pursue more impact-aligned strategies, and so have needed a supporting system for impact analysis. In such cases we have tailored the methodology to the specific needs of the client (according to sector, mission, approach etc.) while retaining the same conceptual architecture. Since its introduction we have tinkered with the methodology along the way, and in 2011 carried out a significant update to incorporate our own growing experience and new developments in the field.

Part II of this book is essentially a MIAA technical manual. It contains the specifics of how the system works, and the individual analytical points that comprise it. Working through these one by one throws up a lot of detail. What follows here is a broad — and much more digestible — overview of the methodology, covering the essential framework, core processes and driving ideas.

Overview

The unit of application of the MIAA is the individual social-purpose organisation,[16] and the opportunity[17] it offers to a capital provider. The aim of the analysis is to furnish the provider with the information and understanding necessary to make an impact-informed decision as to whether or not to put money in.

The salient feature of the MIAA naturally is the address of the organisation's impact. However the impact-focused sections of the analysis must be understood as part of an overall evaluation, which incorporates both social and financial considerations. The fact that these two are brought together and treated in parallel is an important aspect of the MIAA, and one which distinguishes it from the prevalence of "impact only" methodologies, as well as from what could be thought of as the current "default mode" for providers starting to think about impact.

The vast majority of capital providers are well used to applying financial measures when looking at potential investee organisations or applicants for funding, and will typically ask to see annual financial reports, business plans and so on. However as questions about impact are increasingly penetrating the processes used by providers, there is a tendency to separate this side off, and deal with financial due diligence issues as one thing, and concerns around impact as another. Often this leads to the use of separate processes, and potentially separate teams and separate modes of thought. This is problematic on both conceptual and practical levels. In relation to the first, there are considerable dangers to fragmenting analysis as it allows different

---

16   This may be a ground-level organisation carrying out impact-generating activities, or a fund or financing organisation providing capital to such ground-level organisations (e.g. a microfinance fund that invests in but does not itself operate individual microfinance institutions). There is no limit in terms of size, either as to how small or how large, and the MIAA has been applied variously to community charities with turnovers under £100,000, and international funds of $100m.
17   E.g. an investment bond, entry into a fund, equity, project-funding, grant, donation etc..

sets of domain-specific rules to be applied to the different fragments. Each fragment may be treated rationally in and of itself, but the fundamental lack of coherence among them will mean that joining them back together will not necessarily produce a rational result, and conclusions will lack holistic or "big picture" understanding. Indeed the meticulous care taken over the analysis of fragments can overpower what is relatively apparent when looking at the whole, and thus the analytical processes again serve to mystify rather than demystify the decisions they support. Moreover within the social-purpose universe, and for our interests in particular, it would be perverse to accept a total separation of financial and social considerations as this would implicitly run counter to the larger principle of coupling capital with impact.

On a more immediate level, such a separation is unsound analytically as the social and financial sides of social-purpose organisations are demonstrably intertwined. Taken to a logical extreme, an organisation that is financially unviable, and as a result collapses operationally, will likewise collapse with respect to impact. Equally at the other end of the spectrum, an organisation that fails to generate any impact is likely to find that its capitalisation and revenue streams come under threat as impact-seeking clients, funders and investors discover — through transparent and effective impact reporting and analysis — that the social outcomes they sought are not forthcoming.

This is not to say that, when performing an analysis, certain considerations are not clearly related to the financial side (e.g. debt cover ratio) and others to impact (e.g. evidence of beneficiary satisfaction). And accordingly the MIAA comprises two main analytical parts: Confidence, which looks at the financial and operational aspects of the organisation, and Impact, which focuses on the social and environmental benefits. But rather than allowing these two aspects to be treated in isolation, the MIAA brings them together and houses them within a single methodology, by which they are able to stand alongside and mutually inform each other. The subtle interdependence is maintained by an integrated system, with analytical considerations in either part remaining sensitive to an understanding of the other.[18]

---

18 Within Investing for Good, MIAA analyses have always been performed by a single team, with each individual analyst assessing the organisation on both Confidence and Impact fronts. This is the most reliable way to ensure an overall awareness runs through the more specific considerations involved in analysing one or the other. It is however possible to have some analysts focusing more on the financial side and others on impact. What nevertheless remains crucial is that the two are aware of each others' processes and results and work within the same greater structure, and that all analysts are competent with respect to either side.

In addition to the two analytical parts of Confidence and Impact, the MIAA also includes a Mapping stage, which precedes either in the process. Organisations are mapped at the outset in a non-evaluative fashion to classify or tag them with respect to location, sector, size etc., and thereby to form a profile for each organisation. These profiles are assembled into a database which serves three chief functions. Firstly it ensures we are able to organise and indeed analyse the complete body of organisations that have been processed through the MIAA, with the obvious benefits of being able to see what we have looked at and where. Secondly the organisation profiles enable us to match organisations with investors (or other kinds of providers), who are similarly profiled, and so a client looking specifically to invest in e.g. Yorkshire, or renewable energy, or Africa and health, can be presented with a selection of appropriate organisations and opportunities. And thirdly, and most interestingly from the perspective of analysis, the mapping operation supports opportunities for class comparison among different organisations.

Any collection of social-purpose organisations will necessarily make up a multifarious bag, with limited opportunities for one-to-one "best fit" overall comparisons. Comparison among organisations nevertheless remains crucial for a sense of benchmarking and relative performance, and so what the mapping and tagging of organisations facilitates is the formation of specific classes of organisations with respect to particular profile features, and for comparisons to take place within these classes. By this, an organisation may be compared in one class with others of similar size, in another with those working in the same geographic area, in another with those tackling similar social problems, and so on. Each class generates a background field of relevant information and current practice, suggesting to the analyst, for example, commonly measured outcomes and indicators, an appropriate depth and scope for impact reporting, typical results for certain financial ratios, and so on. Thus the database built using the initial mapping stage supports a feel for relative merits in the subsequent stages of analysis and assessment.

Following the Mapping is the evaluative component of the MIAA, comprising the two parts of Confidence and Impact, with Confidence relating to the financial stability of the organisation, and the financial risk implied by providing it with capital; and Impact looking to the positive social and environmental benefits achieved by the organisation through its activities, and thereby through its use of capital. In both parts the analysis is structured around a series of sections, each of which are broken down into sub-sections, and then individual analytical considerations of increasing granularity. The organisation is assessed against these considerations, and is awarded a score on each one. The scores are weighted according to their importance to the overall assessment, and aggregated to arrive at a total for each part: i.e. one total for Confidence, and one for Impact.

The scoring totals are then used to form a rating. The rating relates directly to the social-purpose organisation and the opportunity it offers to a capital provider, and is designed to give a final assessment that is easy to communicate and understand (unlike a raw score of e.g. 63.5), and which gives a "big picture" result.[19] The rating also serves to present the analysis in a format that is readily recognisable to the investment community.

Using predefined bands, the total score for Confidence is translated into a Confidence rating of 1, 2 or 3, with 1 indicating best performance, and likewise the total score for Impact feeds into the Impact rating, again of 1, 2 or 3. These two form two elements within the overall rating, which in the case of impact investments is supplemented with the third element of the prospective financial return. Return is treated as a direct percentage and stands unanalysed and unevaluated (though the Confidence rating does reflect on the anticipated ability of the organisation to achieve its stated return). Including Return ensures the rating covers the three major bases a potential impact investor will want to know about up front — namely: Confidence, Return, and Impact.

CONFIDENCE	RETURN	IMPACT
1 / 2 / 3	x%	1 / 2 / 3
Confidence is a measure of financial confidence in the investment and the underlying organisation. A rating of 1, 2 or 3 is awarded, with 1 indicating best performance.	**Return** indicates the level of financial return offered by the investment, expressed as a percentage. Returns are prospective and may in fact not be realised.	**Impact** is a measure of the organisation's capacity to generate positive social and/ or environmental benefits. A rating of 1, 2 or 3 is awarded, with 1 indicating best performance.

---

19 Results that are phrased in excessively precise terms, like 63.5 or 4.82, tend to invite microlevel discussions that can rapidly become otiose. Also, and especially as a published figure, 63.5 would be meaningful only if it could with confidence be distinguished from a score of 63, or indeed 64. By using a rating, which creates fewer larger distinctions, it is much more feasible to ensure these distinctions remain valid.

The Confidence-Return-Impact rating, or CRI rating, aims to provide an overall view of the organisation and its investment offering, while encouraging investors to look at all three elements. It is critical that the rating encompasses both the Confidence and Impact aspects of the analysis. At the same time, and equally critical, the rating gives distinct expression to each. The MIAA does not support a hybridisation of the two (e.g. by adding or averaging the scores), and rather argues for the inclusion of Impact as a component of investment decision-making in and of itself. This differentiates the methodology and the rating from alternative notions of fully "impact-adjusted" investing, by which, through the use of tools such as Cost Benefit Analysis and hypothesised ROIs, impact is in some way priced directly into the financials. Instead it suggests that impact-informed investing is about being able to understand and balance the two sides.

As with the argument to keep financial Confidence and Impact together in one analytical system, the argument to keep them as separate analytical results responds to both conceptual and practical considerations. Firstly, while in writing the methodology (and this book) we took the position that social impact is a form of social value, and as such is not so very dissimilar to other forms of social value, such as money or risk, and can therefore be measured effectively — this does not imply that measurements of social impact, money, or indeed risk are therefore compatible or combinable. Measuring different things is not the same as reducing them to one thing. Rather, the purpose of the measurement and analysis of impact is to give it an independent and substantive value to place alongside financial values. The MIAA and the CRI rating furnish capital providers with an evaluation on both financial and impact fronts, and it is for providers then to weigh these in relation to their own objectives, as well as their own particular appetite for risk, and — equally importantly — their own particular appetite for impact. As these are likely to be different, there is little to be gained from effecting a forced-conflation of the values involved.

Secondly and on the practical side, efforts to price impact directly, or to collapse it somehow into the financial line, expose impact to the very immediate risk of being mispriced, or for its price to become distorted, inflated, subject to market volatilities and, inevitably, open to questions of confidence. The more the price of a piece of impact jumps around, or is priced incoherently from one market participant to the next, the harder it becomes to convince investors that impact is valid as a price at all, thereby opening the door to a total collapse of the price of impact. Given the nascent state of impact measurement and accounting, and the vastly greater power — not to mention ingenuity — of financial engineering, there is an uncomfortable possibility that investors entering a system on the basis of priced impact, and potentially looking for opportunities for arbitrage, would rapidly overwhelm the mechanisms being used to price that impact.

Cost Benefit Analysis can be a powerful tool, and can serve to illustrate significant aspects of the impact an organisation is achieving. And accordingly, the MIAA incorporates Cost Benefit Analysis considerations into its evaluation (see the summary of Impact below, and the full account given in Part II). These however remain within a particular section of the impact assessment, and do not subsume it, while other sections are assessed in straight impact terms, and remain unmonetised. This unmonetised treatment of impact is carried throughout the process, informed by the understanding that converting impact into a financial value, or a version of a financial value, is probably conceptually unsound; is certainly practically unsound, and consequently liable to misuse; and at heart does not express the information that capital providers most need to know.

A further point a capital provider may however be interested in is the impact of their own specific contribution. When a provider places capital with a social-purpose organisation, that capital (referred to henceforth as the contribution) will have an impact which is clearly connected to — but most likely not the same as — the total impact of that organisation. Its analysis therefore presents a challenge of a related but delicately different kind.

In cases where the contribution finances a specific project or a separate entity (e.g. if the recipient organisation creates a subsidiary to take on new capital and launch a new programme), then normal analytical procedures can be applied to that project or entity in and of itself, and be used to assess its outputs, outcomes and impact independent of the impact of any other activities the organisation may be pursuing. However new financing initiatives are rarely so clean cut, and capital coming into an organisation will often be absorbed into general operations, or used to grow an aspect of operations that is inextricably bound up with the rest of what they do. Compounding this difficulty, well-conceived organisations are likely to be holistic in their activities, with understanding from the various programmes they run feeding back into overall knowledge and strategy, and playing out again into the totality of the impact achieved. This effectively rolls the impact into one, frustrating efforts to separate which aspects of the impact, or how much of it, can be attributed to any particular piece of capital. Thus when a provider looks to assess and potentially aggregate the impact of its own grant-making, lending or investing activities, it has the problem that it is able neither to add the entire impact of the partially-funded organisation to its impact tally, nor to slice out the percentage of that impact that can fairly be said to result from itself.[20]

The MIAA, with its three perspective structure, is designed specifically to achieve an overall view of the organisation (or possible separable entity), and analyse and assess its impact on all fronts. This we believe to be the most cogent and powerful way to approach impact analysis, as well as the way that offers most to the sector as a whole. However in response to the particular need of some providers to be able to address also their own role, we developed an additional analytical section to look at the Impact of Contribution.

Impact of Contribution analysis acts as a kind of bolt-on to the MIAA. Beyond assessment of the organisation's impact upon the world in which it operates, it turns to the particular piece of capital supplied by a provider, and assesses the impact of that contribution upon the organisation. As with other sections of the analysis, a series of analytical considerations are used, each of which are scored and weighted, with the scores again producing a total. This total is kept separate (rather than, for example, being aggregated with the Impact score) on the grounds that Impact of Contribution represents a further parameter by which to understand what a piece of capital is doing in the impact space.

When the Impact of Contribution bolt-on is used,[21] the score is once more translated, via bandings, into a rating element, which forms a further

---

20 This difficulty can contribute, among many other considerations, toward funding bodies choosing to make funds available with specific conditions attached as to what they can be used for. The practice does potentially enforce a degree of discipline upon social-purposes organisations, and help ensure projects are carried out according to the proposal on the basis of which the funds were first offered. However it can also tie up capital, and social-purpose organisations have experienced problems navigating cash-flows among different pieces of restricted funding. Funding tied to particular aspects of what an organisation does also implies impact reporting on those specific areas — i.e. reporting back to the funders on the impacts of the particular funded activities. This leads to organisations with different restricted funding streams having to produce multiple separate impact reports, which can be burdensome. Moreover, as each of these reports is discrete and essentially incomplete regarding the organisation as a whole — not to mention not necessarily public, as it may be made available only to the funder concerned — this form of reporting does not necessarily increase transparency, or help new rounds of funders know more about the impact performance of the underlying organisation. As such it does little to resolve the essential discontinuities that exist within the sector, or work to couple funding with impact in an effective and complete fashion.
21 The use (or not) of the Impact of Contribution bolt-on may vary according to the particular application to which the methodology is being put. For example, for a fund looking to assess its own overall impact, and therefore needing to know the impact of each of the individual impact investments it has made, an Impact of Contribution analysis is highly pertinent. The object of analysis would be in each case the fund's specific contribution. Alternatively, in a review of different impact investment opportunities, structured in multiple forms with various purposes in mind, it is more appropriate to consider the opportunity itself (i.e. the total capital raise) as

ingredient within the overall rating. However as opposed to constituting a 1-2-3 rating in a separate block, the Impact of Contribution result is expressed as a grade of A, B or C, and this grade is placed alongside the 1-2-3 Impact rating as a form of qualifier or sub-rating.

CONFIDENCE	RETURN	IMPACT
1 / 2 / 3	x%	1 / 2 / 3 A/B/C
Confidence is a measure of financial confidence in the investment and the underlying organisation. A rating of 1, 2 or 3 is awarded, with 1 indicating best performance.	**Return** indicates the level of financial return offered by the investment, expressed as a percentage. Returns are prospective and may in fact not be realised.	**Impact** is a measure of the organisation's capacity to generate positive social and/or environmental benefits. A rating of 1, 2 or 3 is awarded, with 1 indicating best performance. A grade of A, B or C is awarded for the **Impact of Contribution**. This is a measure of the relative significance of the capital in question to the organisation's overall activities and impact.

The number-letter combination on Impact thus furnishes a capital provider with information as to both the real impact of the organisation under analysis, and the consequence of the particular piece of capital being dealt with. To give two sketch-examples of how this might work: an Impact rating of 1^C may be awarded to a large organisation with excellent impact that is raising a relatively small volume of working capital.[22] Alternatively, a rating of 2^A may describe an early stage organisation, with comparatively little by way of impact track record (though with a compelling mission and prospective impact chain laid out), that is taking on a major new input of capital in order to scale.

The CRI rating — in its three part form, with the three core elements of Confidence, Return and Impact each represented, and with a grade for the

---

the Contribution being assessed, which an impact investor may or may not wish to take part in by entering (on whatever scale they see fit). For an analysis of social-purpose organisations on an exchange, where opportunities are simply a question of investing in the core capital of one organisation or another, the Impact of Contribution bolt-on may be less relevant, with the full focus resting on the impact of the organisation itself.

22 In such circumstances the organisation may look to a socially-motivated lender. Alternatively the organisation may consider issuing a bond in order to access credit at attractive interest rates essentially through leveraging its social-purpose attributes. As the social sector increasingly engages with different financial products and ways in which to raise capital, more offerings of this kind are likely to enter the marketplace.

Impact of Contribution attached to the Impact element as required — stands as the most concise output of performing a MIAA analysis, and provides, in the clearest and most immediate sense, a result. However the greater value of working through the process, and analysing the organisation in terms of the various sections, subsections and individual scoring considerations, is the information this elicits, and the understanding it generates, as to what the organisation does, and the ways in which it is doing it variously well or less well. In essence, the considerations serve to pull out the key features of the organisation's operations and impact, and call attention to points of excellence or high value, while identifying areas of potential concern or weakness, and gauging how these fit together and into the operational and social context. In the above examples, the Impact rating elements of 1^C or 2^A may offer a piece of the result, but they do not tell the story that the analysis has revealed.

To ensure that the intelligence gained from performing a MIAA analysis is captured along the way, in addition to assigning a score on each consideration, the analyst also attaches a note. And as the scores go toward producing the rating, the notes form the basis for the accompanying impact analysis report. The report offers a critical treatment of the organisation's impact and financial position, and draws on the notes to present the core data and arguments which underpin the rating. The structure of the MIAA is reflected in the structure of the report, which at once ensures an easy transference of information and insight from the analytical process into the analysis report, and provides transparency regarding that process. The report naturally includes the CRI rating, but by supporting it with discourse, gives hair to the otherwise rather bald 1-2-3-style results.

Drawing all this together, a full MIAA analysis therefore comprises:

- a non-evaluative mapping operation
- an evaluative analysis and assessment of Confidence
- an evaluative analysis and assessment of Impact (with an Impact of Contribution bolt-on available as required)

The MIAA outputs are:

- a mapped profile of the organisation (suitable for inclusion in a database and use for class comparison)
- a CRI rating, produced using the Confidence and Impact scores and featuring the prospective financial Return (as well as where appropriate the Impact of Contribution grade)

- an impact analysis report, produced using the notes from the analysis and assessment process, and the intelligence it engenders

These outputs offer in effect a snapshot in time of the organisation and the opportunity it presents to capital providers. The MIAA is however designed for repeat use. Through an annual MIAA analysis and rescoring, it is possible to start charting the organisation's performance through time, with reference both to Confidence and Impact, and to witness any variations taking place. Each MIAA analysis will highlight areas for possible improvement, and successive analyses are thereby able to show whether or not these are being addressed, as well as looking at how new initiatives are influencing performance, and if areas of previous high performance are being maintained. This promises to support improved efficiency and enhanced outcomes for social-purpose organisations and capital providers alike, who both stand to benefit from the gain in clarity, and the opportunities it reveals for informed change (with the concomitant advantages stacking up likewise for beneficiaries, staff and the sector at large). What repeat MIAA analysis also facilitates is for analysts to start observing — both in relation to individual organisations and across the collected body of analysis — the emergence of any potential correlations between Confidence and Impact.[23] This is likely to be of particular interest to those looking to shape the sector, and to grow the social-purpose universe as a whole.

THIS BOOK

Within the MIAA, the part dealing with Impact is far and away the most unique and compelling addition to the field. It is where all the new ideas are concentrated. The Mapping procedure is a fairly standard form of classification. The Confidence assessment consists mostly of established techniques, and is built on the well-paved ground of due diligence, credit analysis, financial statement analysis etc.. These are areas that most capital providers, and many social-purpose organisations, will be comfortably

---

[23] It is possible that correlations emerge also with respect to the financial return, and certainly the MIAA structure and the CRI rating allow for this to be investigated. In the current context however, investments in social-purpose organisations that offer a financial return represent a small minority of the sector's — and often of individual organisations' — overall capitalisation. As a result of this, financial returns are often more indicative of how one or another organisation has decided to structure and market its investment offering, and less to do with the fundamentals of its operations. As such, for the time being at least, we believe it is less likely that correlations with Return will be observable.

INVESTING FOR GOOD

familiar with. What this book — and almost certainly its readers — are really interested in is the treatment of Impact.

This overview aims to lay out the structure of the MIAA, and the thinking behind that structure, including the integral role that Mapping and Confidence play within the overall process. However, for the purposes of the rest of this book, the focus is firmly on Impact. What follows is a brief summary of the Mapping and Confidence components, and then a much fuller account of how the Impact analysis works. Chapter 4. On Using the MIAA describes a little the experience of putting the MIAA into practice, and discusses the lessons learned and results produced. Part II, Methodology for Impact Analysis and Assessment (MIAA) then sets out the Impact component of the MIAA in full.[24] Part III, Guidelines for How to Measure and Report Social Impact provides the Guidelines for social-purpose organisations.

---

24 The Mapping and Confidence components are not reproduced in full for two main reasons. Firstly, and as noted above, they are fairly standard in nature, and so to publish them would add more to the bulk than to the content of this book, and likewise to the existing body of knowledge (there is after all no great shortage of sources of financial analysis tools). Secondly, and as also touched on above, most capital providers and actors in the social-purpose universe already have their own sets of financial questions and markers in place, as well as profiling operations, and these will have been designed specifically for their own interests and purposes (which may vary considerably — an investor, a commissioner and a grant-maker, for example, are likely to have different takes on what they want to see in terms of financials). The arguments made above regarding the integration of Confidence and Impact in the MIAA do not suggest that the financial systems currently in use among capital providers need be redesigned completely, nor that an analysis of Confidence must adhere to a prescribed set of measures. Rather the case is that Confidence analysis of some kind (and of whatever kind is most appropriate for the organisation or capital provider in question) is important, and it is further important that this analysis is performed alongside the analysis of Impact (e.g. it is done by the same team or communicating teams), and that the two are treated together as part of an overall analysis. The microlevel specifics of our particular Confidence toolkit however, and the details of our Mapping operation, are not absolute desiderata, nor things upon which the ideas driving the Impact part of the analysis hang. To lay them out in full therefore seemed potentially to present more of a distraction than a contribution.

Mapping

Mapping is the first stage of the MIAA analysis, and creates a simple profile that sits in a database of mapped and MIAA-analysed organisations. The database supports the most fundamental aspects of being able to order, sort and understand the mapped sections of the social-purpose universe, as well as allowing clients to be matched with organisations, and organisations to be matched with each other for analytical class comparison.

The table sets out the main sections of the Mapping operation.

MAPPING
Organisation
including: name of organisation, mission, sector, products or services, business model
Location
including: location of headquarters, location of operations and impacts, if the organisation is UK-focused or international
Scale and Stage of Development
including: total assets, turnover, years of operating history
Investment Opportunity
including: size of capital raise, scale ratio (capital raise / total assets), type of investment (debt, equity), investment term, liquidity, date of close (or open ended)
Impact
including: impact target, directness of impact, presence of impact report, unequivocal primacy of mission

INVESTING FOR GOOD

Confidence

The Confidence part of the analysis is comprised of a series of sections and subsections, each breaking down into individual scoring considerations, which drill into the operational and financial viability of the organisation, as well as its exposure to risk and its future prospects. This involves scrutiny of the organisation itself and of the sector in which it operates — and of the structure and stability of the specific (investment) opportunity it is offering to capital providers. The various sections largely correspond to areas of company analysis in a commercial context, though are tailored to certain specific conditions of the social sector. For example, social-purpose organisations often have comparatively little experience of debt or investment, may have limited historical data, and be operating in fields that are themselves relatively new or untested (indeed the majority of impact investments would count as high risk in conventional financial circles). This therefore requires a greater sensitivity to such factors as the systems and strategies the organisation has in place, and the resources it has access to, as well as to the organisation's managerial strength and board expertise, and potential affiliations with larger more established organisations. Certain social-sector-specific risks feature, such as policy risk (e.g. for organisations reliant on supplying social services to local authorities) and country risk (e.g. for organisations working in potentially unstable parts of the developing world).

The table sets out the main sections of the Confidence analysis and assessment.

CONFIDENCE
Scale and Structure
including analysis of the scale and structure of both the organisation and of the capital raise
Narrative
including analysis of the history and track record of the organisation, and of its prospective future (covering strategy and business plan)
Operational Strength
including analysis of the organisation's systems, procedures and non-financial resources, and of its financial viability (covering income, cash flow, assets and liabilities, reserves, and relations with funders, clients and commissioners)

Communication and Transparency
including analysis of the organisation's reporting and general communication and presentation of itself
Management and Staff
including analysis of the board, executive team and relations with staff
Diversification
including analysis of geographical and operational diversification, and diversity of income streams and sources of capital
Sector Risks
including analysis of sector growth and competition, as well as the organisation's planned response to sector risks and opportunities
Policy Risk
including analysis of the organisation's exposure (either direct or indirect) to changes in government policy, and, where appropriate, of measures taken by the organisation to manage such risks
Country Risk
including analysis of the organisation's exposure to risks regarding potentially unstable countries, currencies or environments, and, where appropriate, of measures taken by the organisation to manage such risks

Impact

The Impact part of the analysis takes a multidimensional approach, structuring itself around three key perspectives. These represent the three major positions that surround the creation and experience of impact, and are: the social-purpose organisation generating the impact; the beneficiary receiving the impact; and the world beyond the organisation and its direct beneficiaries into which the impact is ultimately absorbed. Correspondingly the methodology is divided into three sections, each of which can be characterised by a perspectival question:

1. Mission-Fulfilment
   With respect to the organisation's own mission, to what extent is that mission being effectively fulfilled by the organisation's activities and operations?

2. Beneficiary Perspective
   To what extent are beneficiaries experiencing positive change in their lives as a result of the organisation's activities?

3. Wider Impact
   How is the change playing out in wider contexts and environments, and what are the implications for local and societal benefits?

As with Confidence, these sections are each broken down into subsections and sets of analytical considerations, each with a weighted score.

The tripartite approach with its three underlying perspectives has two effects in terms of how the analysis works. Firstly, by investigating the three positions independently, the analysis is able to look at each in detail, and cover the full range of ways and areas in which an organisation may be generating positive social value, either directly or following on from its activities. This aims to fulfil the first challenge facing a methodology — namely that it can pick up and score all the different kinds of impact being generated. Secondly, the three perspectives serve to verify and corroborate each other. If the organisation is generating social value, this value should not only be picked up by at least one perspective, but may be observable from two or three. For example, a high value impact may feature prominently with respect to the organisation's mission, in the lives of beneficiaries, and in the local community. Conversely impacts that are apparent from one or two perspectives may score well within their sections, especially if they penetrate deeply, but the structure of the methodology and the nature of the corroboration effect is such that organisations that are able to evidence impacts across all three fronts automatically score more highly. This addresses the two remaining principle challenges for a methodology. Firstly, corroboration provides protection against bias, or the overvaluing of a particular element, as singular impacts that are apparent from only one perspective are naturally limited in terms of their scoring potential. And secondly, by almost the same token, impacts that do score highly do so only through being corroborated and verified from several positions, thus ensuring they are valid, and that the value attributed to them by the analysis is robust and defensible.

The following section by section outlines lay out the way in which the analysis and assessment is structured with respect to each of the three perspectives.

MISSION FULFILMENT

Mission Fulfilment focuses on the social-purpose organisation itself. This starts with looking to the organisation's mission statement, and analysing the validity and coherence of its approach with respect to that mission. Taken together, the mission and approach are regarded as stronger when supported by a clear understanding of the problems or issues the organisation is tackling, and the focus and scope of its own operations.

Following this, the methodology turns to the organisation's ability to demonstrate how it is furthering its mission and the impact it is having. This necessarily involves looking to the organisation's engagement with impact measurement. Referring to the basic framework laid out in the standard model (outlined above in 2. Analysing Analysis), the organisation is assessed for its use of an effective impact measurement system, with considerations covering the cogency of the impact chain, the presence of well-defined outputs and outcomes, the use of indicators to track these, and the reporting of results.[25]

Organisations that do not engage in any kind of impact measurement, and are able to produce very little by way of information about what they are doing and achieving, inevitably score poorly. If the analyst is unable to find

---

25 Organisations may not themselves use this specific language — indeed the lack of a standardised vocabulary is one of the issues impact measurement and analysis continues to face. However the concepts remain consistent at the system level, and a skilled analyst will be able to recognise the organisation's impact chain, outputs etc., even if the organisation has not explicitly used these terms or drawn these structures out itself.

any information relating to a particular consideration, either in published reporting or through direct contact, then a default score of zero is awarded on that line. This is justified on the grounds that a lack of transparency or evidence around impact compromises confidence in both the impact itself and in the organisation's ability to achieve impact (on the basis of the aforementioned argument that organisations that don't really know what they are achieving are unlikely to be achieving it all that well). It also relates to the needs of socially-motivated capital providers, who irrespective of whether or not they are expecting a financial return, will be looking for a social return of some kind. If the organisation is not able to demonstrate its delivery of social impact in a meaningful way, then the idea of the social return rather collapses in on itself. A direct product of this "no-information-score-zero" rule within the methodology is that — as organisations that measure and report upon impact are able to pick up points more easily, and therefore score higher, achieve higher ratings, and become more attractive to capital — there is a clear incentive for organisations to engage with impact reporting. This of course is in line with the thrust of what we are trying to achieve (see above 1. Measure in Everything), and the core concept of coupling capital deployment with tangible social impact.

Having considered the organisation for its use of impact measurement, the analysis naturally proceeds to look at the actual results produced by such measurement, and to assess performance. Again this assessment is from the perspective of the organisation itself, and so looks to the organisation's targets and objectives, and addresses whether or not it is carrying out its planned activities efficiently, whether or not these are proving effective (i.e. producing the intended results), and so on. Importantly the results are referred back to the organisation's original mission, and the progress it is making toward its stated goals.

Finally the results are considered for how they are feeding back into the organisation and informing the impact plan for the future. Notably, in its use of new information, and in relation to the successes and failures of its different activities, analysis asks: is the organisation responsive, is it flexible, is it looking to improve, and are there signs that going forwards it is growing its impact?

BENEFICIARY PERSPECTIVE

The Beneficiary Perspective looks at impact specifically from the point of view of the impact target, and investigates the value of the change experienced by beneficiaries. This idea of change relates not to the intended effect as defined by the social-purpose organisation (or associated levels of accomplishment, as in Mission Fulfilment), but to a more absolute idea of social value, and how it can be unlocked by change. Essentially what is being asked is: what is the change in the beneficiary's life, and what is that change worth? As such, the Beneficiary Perspective assessment stands outside of the standard model of impact chains and reporting mechanisms, which are all specific to their organisations and particular fields, and relates instead to a continuous concept for the value of change. It is as such the boldest part of the methodology.

Analysis is broken into two subsections, each representing a relationship: firstly the relationship between the beneficiary and the social-purpose organisation (from the beneficiary perspective), termed Beneficiary Focus; and secondly the relationship between the beneficiary and the change, termed Beneficiary Impacts.

Beneficiary Focus
The beneficiary focus assessment acts as a check to ensure that the target beneficiaries are indeed being reached, engaged and included in the organisation's activities.

In the past, models for philanthropy and development programmes have tended toward a normative approach. By this, the organisation making the intervention determines the methods and goals, both of which are based primarily on the intervening organisation's experience and beliefs. Thus the intervention will tend to seek to normalise beneficiaries toward the position of the intervener. Historically the most obvious examples of this have come from Western development organisations pushing Western-style ideas or behaviours in developing countries (e.g. through delivering aid, equipment etc. in a *deus ex machina* fashion) without fully investigating whether or not these are, in context, appropriate, workable, or likely to be adopted. Over recent years the flaws in this method, and increasing criticism of a "one size fits all" approach, have led to a growing recognition of the importance of the beneficiary perspective. As ultimately it is the life of the beneficiary that the intervention is hoping to have a positive impact upon, the beneficiary's compliance is crucial not only for ethical or democratic reasons, but also for practical ones. Mobilising beneficiary interest and initiative is key to the success of any social-purpose organisation, as almost all impacts will require a degree of investment on the part of beneficiaries too — often financial, and commonly also investments of labour, time, and creative energy. In order to secure this, and ensure meaningful and sustaining impacts, awareness of beneficiaries is vital. This requires a dynamic bilateral relationship between the organisation and its beneficiaries, with information and understanding flowing in both directions.

In the previous section, analysis of Mission Fulfilment covered such questions as whether or not the organisation can define its beneficiaries, and if it knows who they are, understands their context and so on (this comes under analysis of mission, scope and focus). But it is equally important for beneficiaries to know about the organisation. Accordingly Beneficiary Focus assessment looks first to establish that beneficiaries are aware of the organisation, and are able to access its services in an inclusive (i.e. non-discriminatory) fashion.

Following this, consideration is given to whether beneficiaries are able to express their ideas to the organisation (typically evidenced by some form of consultation), and whether they are being engaged in processes, and empowered thereby. This may take the form of beneficiary participation in activities, or the planning of activities, or having a role within decision-making or defining goals or parameters. Through these and other forms of engagement, the key point is that the way in which impact is being generated is open to beneficiary input.

Beneficiary participation is of particular interest to the analyst as, in addition to being democratic and effective as a process, it provides a clear indication of a beneficiary-side sense of value. While activities which fail to engage beneficiaries may risk being misdirected, the presence of beneficiaries working actively with the organisation gives an implicit beneficiary-perspective vote of confidence in favour of the approach and of the impacts being achieved.

The final area of analysis for Beneficiary Focus is to look at the extent to which beneficiaries are being supported to communicate with each other and form mutually empowering networks. Through their outreach and services, organisations are often able to bring together beneficiaries who suffer from exclusion or disadvantage in some way. They are thus in a position to leverage further social value by helping those beneficiaries to connect — either directly with each other, or by threading together information and experience from different beneficiaries, and making this knowledge more generally available.

Beneficiary Impacts

The Beneficiary Impacts section then turns to the actual changes experienced by beneficiaries as a result of the organisation's activities, and seeks to analyse how profound these changes are. The essential point at stake is: how much better are beneficiaries' lives being made?

In many ways this is the single most important question for the entire sector. Ultimately the goal of any social-purpose organisation is for its beneficiaries to feel positive social value coming into their lives. And the experience of this value — from the beneficiary perspective — is necessarily the most meaningful, tangible and relevant expression of social impact. However, because of the obvious challenges it presents to measurement, it is also the area most commonly circumvented by measurement systems. Traditionally social-purpose organisations have instead treated the question of how much better the lives of their beneficiaries are through a form of narrative metonymy, by which the story of one or perhaps a few beneficiaries are told, and these then stand for the whole.

In order to arrive at a fuller and more analytical treatment of Beneficiary Impacts, a more structured understanding of what a change for a beneficiary actually is, and how it relates to the organisation, is required.

In essence, social-purpose organisations identify people whose lives are in some sense compromised — often through exclusion from certain resources, services or advantages — and seek to redress that compromise through their activities. The first point for evaluation therefore is how severely compromised is the beneficiary's experience of life before any redress takes place? This is a complicated matter as it veers toward ethics and away from objective analysis, with potentially endless corridors of discourse opening up as to what constitutes a severe compromise, what a mild compromise, can what for one person is mild perhaps for another be severe, how in this context are "mild" and "severe" to be understood, and so on. However, while a philosophically complete treatment is unlikely ever to be arrived at, very significant progress has been made in this direction in the field of human rights. Through research and cooperation, workable definitions as to what constitutes an infringement of an individual's essential humanity have been developed, laid down, refined over decades, and during that time, won considerable international recognition and adoption. Human rights as a discipline thus offers two things. Firstly, a level of maturity and exposure on a big stage (something impact measurement as a practice lacks). Ideas about human rights have been rigorously tested and applied all over the world under conditions of heavy legal and media scrutiny, and have through this developed in toughness. Secondly, support for and — equally importantly — input into a contemporary understanding of human rights, has come from both developed and developing world countries. This endows human rights frameworks with a certain inner legitimacy, as while a degree of normalisation is implied (i.e. normalisation to a single standard of human rights), this standard is based on a common sense of humanity rather than on a particular cultural heritage or any one ideology. One of the key innovations of the MIAA is to draw on existing thinking about human rights and the accompanying body of research, and apply it to the assessment of Beneficiary Impacts.

A human rights approach focuses on the extent to which people are able to exercise control over their own lives, and make unencumbered decisions about their future. Human rights in this sense denotes not only basic notions of freedom from torture or political oppression, but also rights to development, rights to well-being and education, rights to live within a healthy and sustainable environment, and so on. These rights play into each other and connect to form the essential human infrastructure through which people are able to experience freedom in a comprehensive and meaningful fashion.

Rights in this sense can not only be violated, but also constrained by circumstances, such as those frequently endured by disadvantaged or excluded people. The impact of an organisation may thus be framed as advancing the access of its beneficiaries to those human rights which, in the absence of its intervention, are experienced in a compromised fashion, or not at all. Adopting this framework, Beneficiary Impacts analysis is able to take a structured approach to the beneficiaries in question, and identify which human rights stood compromised before the impact, and gauge the extent to which these rights are enjoyed in a fuller fashion as a result of the impact. The degree of enhanced access to human rights is effectively a measure of the depth of change to beneficiaries' lives.

In terms of the mechanics of assessment, this translates into a matrix of human, social and environmental rights. The matrix is composed of fifteen core social and environmental fields (e.g. education, employment, housing), and attached to each of these are certain prominent indicators that serve to highlight the different ways in which beneficiaries are typically able to realise enhanced access to rights within these fields. The organisation's impacts are analysed in relation to each one, with the indicators serving to identify where gains are being made. These are then reviewed in total to provide a picture of the overall change. Different organisations will, according to their missions, find more or less resonance in different areas of the matrix, most likely achieving a strong address in one or two fields.

It is important to note however that human rights — and so the fields within the matrix — are fundamentally indivisible. For example, the right to education plays into improved access to a host of subsequent rights, such as those to employment and to participation in political and cultural life. Equally, for an organisation focused on job creation, the most obvious human rights gain is in the right to employment, but through supporting beneficiaries in finding work, significant further advances are likely to be forthcoming in other areas, such as in the right to financial security, and in enhanced beneficiary confidence, an aspect of the right to well-being. Conversely compromised rights, for example to the highest attainable standard of health, can pass outwards to effect compromises on multiple other fronts, such as access to education and employment. Advancing a beneficiary's right to reasonable housing and a sustainable human environment may well yield benefits with respect to health rights, and so on.

What rapidly becomes apparent when performing analysis using a matrix of human, social and environmental rights is that deep level changes result in a wide range of enhancements. The holistic nature of human rights ensures that a major impact upon one human right resonates powerfully across numerous others, resulting in improved access to multiple rights. Relatively shallow or light interventions on the other hand are unlikely to lead to significant benefits elsewhere, and so show up more patchily. This supports the process of assessing and scoring Beneficiary Impacts using the matrix, as the highest impact interventions — i.e. those which lead to comprehensive change throughout beneficiaries' lives — present themselves on multiple scoring lines, thus automatically picking up more points than lower impact interventions, which lack this degree of resonance. As with the corroboration effect across the three perspectives, the resonant quality of rights within the matrix provides the analytical structure with an in-built means to assign higher scores to more substantial impacts. As such, the matrix provides an effective tool for looking at social impacts of any kind, relating them to an essential framework for humanity, and gauging the profundity or depth of change produced as experienced by the individual beneficiary.

The corollary to this kind of depth of change analysis, for an assessment of the organisation's overall Beneficiary Impact, is then to look at the breadth of change, and ask: how widely is this change being rolled out? Using the changes identified through the matrix analysis as points of reference, assessment looks to the number of beneficiaries experiencing these changes. This is sometimes referred to as the number of "lives touched."

To ensure however that this doesn't merely become a reflection of the scale of the organisation, the number of lives touched needs to be considered in relation to the organisation's size, and so rather than a question of total breadth the consideration is one of breadth efficiency. From the point of view of capital allocation, this efficiency is necessarily seen in relation to the volume of capital required to leverage that breadth, in effect producing the notion of "unit cost."

In its simplest form, unit cost is a ratio of money in to lives touched, or "dollars per life touched". However a slightly more nuanced approach is required. A sense of the organisation's capital intensity can be gained from its turnover, but the total assets also need to be taken into account, especially if these are large and impose a potential limit to growth (without further correspondingly large injections of capital). The figure for lives touched most obviously relates to the number of unique beneficiaries receiving services, though this needs to be cross referenced with the actual number who are experiencing change, and also needs to be sensitive to environmental factors and benefits. Prevailing sector ratios may be useful for gaining a sense of the organisation's efficiency in this regard, and this is a particular area where the development of benchmarks has much to offer.

WIDER IMPACT

The third perspective from which the organisation's impact is assessed is the world beyond the organisation itself and its immediate beneficiaries — i.e. a "surrounding" or "whole world" perspective, which is looked at in terms of the Wider Impact.

The first point to be considered in relation to the organisation's impact in the wider environment is that of additionality. The elementary concept of impact is of something (a force, an intervention, a set of activities) hitting something else (a particular environment), and that something else being different as a consequence — i.e. the collision has effected a change. The impact should therefore be apparent when comparing the "before" and "after" situations. But to be truly additional, it is necessary to consider also what the situation would have been like had the impact not taken place. For a completely static system this needn't be a concern because the default is for it to stay the same. For example, if an asteroid hits the surface of the moon, it is reasonably safe to assume that had it missed, the surface would have looked much as it did before. This however very much isn't the case on earth, and especially in social situations, where things are in constant flux, and in the absence of one thing happening, something else is likely to occur. The question that arises therefore is: how would things look if the impact hadn't taken place — i.e. if the asteroid hadn't hit? Thinking about this calls up a kind of business-as-usual (BAU) scenario, sometimes in this context referred to as the "counterfactual case", or "what would have happened anyway."

The BAU scenario, in relation to the impact of social-purpose organisations in the wider world, poses the question: what would happen in the wider world if the organisation did not exist? Comparing the theoretical BAU scenario with the observed situation — i.e. the one including the organisation and its impact — indicates the additionality of that impact. Additionality is the change that stands over and above any changes that would otherwise have taken place.

There are two critical ways in which an organisation's impact may be compromised by additionality considerations. Firstly, it may be that an organisation is providing services which, were they not to exist, beneficiaries would simply arrange for themselves. For example, an organisation focused on employment may find jobs for a particular number of beneficiaries, but to be truly additional it is important that these beneficiaries would not have found jobs on their own. Similarly, for a programme working with ex-offenders, additionality asks not only what is the reoffending rate achieved with the programme, but what is the reoffending rate that could be expected in the absence of the programme.[26]

This aspect of additionality effectively compares an intervention to a no-intervention scenario, with the expectation that, unless the organisation's activities are essentially ill-targeted, there should be significant additionality present.[27] The second aspect of additionality to consider however is whether, in the absence of the organisation performing its intervention, another organisation would have been active in its place. This may be the case for example with suppliers of social services to local authorities, where contracts for the services stand irrespective, and are necessarily fulfilled even if you take a particular organisation away. Competition or crowding may also affect additionality in a similar way if, for example, the organisation is active in a well-supplied context, in which beneficiaries may be accessing services from one organisation, but could in its absence go elsewhere. This is not to discredit the activities of organisations working with contracts or in busy and competitive sectors, but it does distinguish them on this front from organisations pioneering wholly new or undersupplied services, who thus unlock benefits that otherwise would not have been available. Such organisations are, on this specific measure, considered higher impact.

---

26 To demonstrate additionality over the BAU scenario, organisations may refer to research showing what the BAU looked like prior to their activities, or what it looks like in other comparable areas where they are not active. Being hypothetical, the case of what would have happened without the organisation in the organisation's own field of operations has necessarily to be guessed at. However compelling evidence from sensibly chosen parallels can be used to present a clear case for the additionality of the intervention. Increasingly sophisticated techniques, including the use of Randomised Control Trials, are migrating from academia into practice, and enabling researchers, analysts and organisations alike to construct convincing and even experimental evidence as to what the additionality of an impact really is.

27 The true impact may need to be recalibrated slightly in accordance with this aspect of the BAU. For example, if 10% of beneficiaries could typically be expected to achieve the same outcomes without the support of the organisation, the impact is 90% additional.

A final aspect of additionality to look to is the potential cost benefits to the wider world as a result of the organisation's work. These may include the increased economic productivity of beneficiaries following engagement with the organisation, for example through being in work, being healthier, being more able etc.. There may also be significant cost savings — in terms of direct state expenditure (e.g. social benefits no longer being drawn, health costs no longer being imposed etc.); or through the avoidance of costly negative scenarios (e.g. beneficiaries no longer reoffending, with the implied savings to society in terms of judicial costs, damage to locality etc.).

As touched upon earlier (see Overview above), this particular concept of the costs benefits of an organisation's impact, or its "net present value" in economic terms, is one that has received considerable attention — not least because it has the allure of a clean number result, and moreover one that can be expressed in financial terms. And indeed a careful and legitimate working through of the cost benefits of an organisation's work can provide a powerful argument, especially to government (to whom the cost benefits mostly accrue) in favour of giving financial support to an organisation's activities. However cost benefits should not be confused with impact. There are significant forms of impact which offer little by way of cost benefits — or, more likely, costs benefits that are too removed and diluted among other factors to be calculated sensibly. Cost benefits are one potential aspect of an organisation's impact within the wider context in which it operates, and so make up one subsection within the methodology, but do not by any means overwhelm it.

Beyond the question of additionality and the social and economic gains made over the BAU scenario, analysis of Wider Impact looks at ways in which the organisation's direct impacts are multiplying as they pass outwards into the surrounding context, creating further benefits as they go. This applies most immediately to economic multipliers, whereby money feeding into the local or beneficiary economy as a result of the organisation's activities may be onspent and respent within that economy, each time boosting local GDP. The organisation may also multiply up its contribution to the local economy by leveraging further investment (e.g. if other companies, institutions or state bodies are moved to invest in the area or sector), or by contributing to a general rise in local value as a result of improving conditions (observed e.g. through a rise in property values).

Alongside economic multipliers, there may also be a form of knowledge multiplication, by which the organisation's concerns and ideas pass on throughout the wider context, effecting further change. Knowledge multiplication of this kind may happen: within the particular sector in which the organisation operates (e.g. through sharing knowledge with other organisations); with government or business (e.g. through campaigning and representation); and with the public (e.g. through raising public awareness).

Beyond multiplication of direct knowledge, the organisation may be able to create a game change in prevailing dynamics, either through innovating a wholly new approach, or through pioneering existing models or concepts in new areas. The key indication of game change is seen as the organisation breaking new ground in a way that inspires other organisations to follow.

In addition to analysing the ways in which the impact influences the wider context, it is important also to look to how the wider context may affect the impact, and in particular how it may threaten the impact. This in effect is a consideration of the risk to the impact. The impact's sustainability may be threatened typically if the organisation's impacts are concentrated in a narrow region or field and liable to being replaced (e.g. by a new model or technology), or if they are overly dependent on a particular policy environment which likewise may change.

The final consideration within Wider Impact analysis turns to the organisation's internal processes, and the impact it has on its own staff, volunteers, and the environment. These concerns relate to the principles of responsible management (e.g. the presence of fair employment policies, engagement with environmentally sustainable practices etc.), and as such do not necessarily affect the organisation's primary mission or target beneficiaries. They are essentially secondary to the major question of what impact the organisation is able to achieve through doing what it does. Nevertheless they are a part of the organisation's wider impact, and are therefore addressed in the closing section. Analysis on this front is derived from a relatively standard set of principles for corporate social responsibility.

IMPACT OF CONTRIBUTION (BOLT-ON)

The final section of the impact-orientated part of the analysis is the Impact of Contribution bolt-on. This relates essentially to the perspective of the capital provider in asking: what is the impact of the capital contribution in question to the social-purpose organisation? As such it does not address the organisation's social impact directly, hence its position outside of the main Impact analysis and assessment. Rather it is a tool to help capital providers understand the impact of their own funding and investing activities.

Analysis of Impact of Contribution is broken down into four main areas. The first and most obvious is that of the scale of the contribution — i.e. the volume of new capital being injected in comparison with the size of the organisation itself (taking into account both its turnover and its fixed assets, and how the new capital is to be used). Secondly there is the question of the leverage of the contribution, which looks to any structural role it might be playing in terms of the organisation's financing, and whether the organisation has been able to use it to raise further capital. Thirdly, consideration is given to the organisation's financial management and planning. Here the contribution may have had an influence in such areas as improving financial discipline, or inspiring the organisation to think in new ways about how it accesses and uses capital. Providers may themselves play a pivotal role in this by offering additional financial or business advice. Then fourthly, analysis looks to the organisational growth stimulated by the contribution. Consideration is given to ways in which the capital is facilitating new revenue-generating activities that enhance the organisation's operational viability and self-sustainability, and feed into an expansion of activities and thereby impact. A further point of analysis in the case of contributions that have already been made, and are being reviewed, is the organisation's use of the contribution, and the question of whether the capital has indeed been put to work as intended, and is — directly or indirectly — driving impact.

For tables and detailed notes setting out the analysis and assessment of Impact in full, see Part II, Methodology for Impact Analysis and Assessment (MIAA).

4. ON USING THE MIAA

The impact methodology outlined above, comprising the three key sections of Mission Fulfilment, Beneficiary Perspective and Wider Impacts, is aimed at analysing and assessing the organisation and its impact in its entirety. The three sections are positioned to capture information relating to any aspect of potential impact generation, and having captured it, the analyst is then able to scrutinise and evaluate it, and award points accordingly. Totalling these points produces a score for the overall impact, which is then translated, via defined scoring bands, into the rating.

There are a number of implications to this process which rapidly become apparent when using it. Firstly, as the methodology and the considerations that comprise it are designed to cover all forms of impact, it is likely that many will not be relevant to any one organisation. Unless the organisation is active on every front, there will be scoring lines which search for forms of impact that it is not achieving, and on which it will therefore score zero. This in itself is not a problem as a high performing organisation will score well in other areas, and thus still be able to pick up the points required to finish in the top band of the ratings. In this way it is important to conceive of the score less as a percentage — e.g. 76% of impact achieved, with an implied 24% of impact missing or failing to be achieved — and more as an aggregate — e.g. an aggregate of 84 impact points scored in these particular areas, equating to a rating of 1. As the organisation under analysis is passed through the different considerations, these in effect present it with multiple opportunities to score points and build a successful aggregate, but with no burden of expectation to attain perfect scores throughout.

At the same time, an important part of the process is that it does indicate where the organisation is not achieving impact (or doing little to evidence its impact), and while this may simply be due to particular considerations not being relevant to the organisation's approach, it may equally be due to weaknesses in the organisation's impact performance. In this way the methodology is able to flag up gaps or holes in the impact, and as the analyst works through the considerations and applies each one, areas of deficiency are progressively revealed. Ultimately more holes where the organisation should be scoring points will lead to a lower aggregate and an inferior rating.

Used in this fashion, the methodology acts a little like a checklist. It is an effective and systematic way to ensure the analyst asks all the right questions of an organisation when performing an analysis. By incorporating

INVESTING FOR GOOD

a weighted scoring system, it further provides the analyst with a consistent means to gauge the importance of these questions and arrive at a rating. And while the scores find expression in the rating, the actual answers to the questions generate the informational content and evaluative insights that make up the impact analysis report.

MIAA IN USE

The MIAA was first assembled as an explicit methodology in 2009, and has since then been subject to further tuning as well as an overall update in 2011. During that time, over one hundred social-purpose organisations and investment opportunities have been processed through it and analysed, rated and had reports written about them. In addition to this the methodology has underpinned our impact consultancy services to other organisations. The rest of this chapter offers some observations upon the methodology in use, as well as addressing a few of the questions most frequently asked when we present it.

The first test for the MIAA upon its initial introduction into practice was a basic one of operational feasibility. Essentially: how time-consuming and how expensive in terms of human resources would it be to perform such an analysis? On this front, we found that once analysts were familiar with the methodology, the process of analysing an organisation, scoring it and preparing a report would represent two to three days work, which we felt was reasonable and appropriate. What could however significantly extend the process were delays in extracting information from organisations under analysis. Organisations could sometimes be slow to respond, and potentially incomplete in their response, making it harder to gather the data needed to perform a full analysis, and thus presenting an additional time cost.[28] However we anticipate that as impact reporting and analytical procedures become increasingly prevalent and standardised throughout the sector, difficulties of this kind will tail off.

It is worth noting in relation to gathering information that the analyses we performed relied heavily upon material supplied to us by the organisations under analysis. The scoring system does reward the provision of audited social reports and convincing external evidence of impact, but these are

---

28   Ultimately if an organisation is unable to divulge any relevant information for a particular consideration the default score of zero is awarded. This is on the basis that a lack of transparency undermines confidence (in both Confidence and Impact), and takes away from the concept of a deliverable social return.

not mandatory,[29] and we did not perform independent checks upon the impact of our own. Contact between the analysis team and the organisation would lead to meetings (often in person or if not via telephone) to discuss points brought up by the analysis, and this would simultaneously act as a first layer of scrutiny and testing for trust. However the process could be made more complete by thorough onsite visits to organisations under analysis, including engagement in greater "impact due diligence" and investigations to confirm the organisation's published or provided data. Ultimately not doing this for all or a sample of organisations was a resourcing issue.

Beyond feasibility — and more intriguing — was the question of the consistency of results. To test this, when we first devised the methodology we engaged four interns (MSc students in Finance and Accounting at LSE) to enter into a process of analysing organisations independently and then meeting to compare scores. Over the first few meetings minor confusions over the meaning of certain considerations and points of language were ironed out, and the interns gained in confidence and competence with growing familiarity with the sector and the methodology itself. With this came considerable convergence in the scores awarded as well as in the notes made and the arguments formed as to the strengths and weaknesses of a particular organisation's impact. Convergence also derived from a peer-generated sense of "fair scoring," with initially harsher and more generous scorers gravitating toward each other over the iterative process (comparative agreement as to which organisations were higher or lower in impact was apparent from the start). This indicated that the MIAA was capable of producing consistent — and consistently reasoned — scores, but that a lack of explicitly defined benchmarks meant that learning where to pitch scores was in part about finding internal benchmarks (i.e. developing a sense of what good and poor performance in the sector looks like), and in part a process of "social benchmarking" (i.e. finding a common feel for scoring within a peer group of analysts), rather than relying entirely on rigorously defined external factors. One of the improvements we have since

---

29   Over the 2009–2011 period leading into writing this book, externally verified impact reporting was very much the exception rather than the norm among social-purpose organisations, and indeed had the methodology demanded it, there simply would have been very few organisations or investment opportunities to analyse. We believe this will continue to be the case for some years to come, and while the concept of organisations producing fully audited social reports has attractive aspects, the current levels of infrastructure and investment of resources toward this goal keep it beyond the reach of the foreseeable future. However accreditation of process and reporting, as a less intensive form of third party validation, is a more tangible possibility for widespread uptake. Various forms of accreditation are available already (e.g. SROI, B-Lab), and it is likely more will be developed and supported over the coming years.

made to the MIAA is to create clearer guidelines as to what constitutes a high, medium or low score on any particular consideration. Beyond this, moving toward stipulated and, in certain areas, sector-specific benchmarks remains an ongoing challenge for the social-purpose universe. Again this is a space where we anticipate that the growing engagement with impact measurement and the publication of more results will lead to significant progress in the near to medium-term future.

Following from this initial test, in implementing the MIAA into operational use we have continued to follow a similar process for training analysts in the application of the methodology, by which two or more analysts parallel-score the same organisation and meet to compare results in the presence of an experienced analyst. Once a reasonable level of consistency of understanding and scoring is reached, analysts may then start to score organisations independently. Each rating and accompanying report produced in this way is then reviewed in house by a social impact committee, and sent back past the organisation under analysis for approval (and further review if need be) before being signed off. We believe the ratings and reports produced in this way are valid and robust, and stand together in a consistent relationship with one another, with their underlying organisations, and with a meaningful concept of social impact.

What the ratings are able to say about rated organisations is necessarily a reflection of the state of the social-purpose universe, and the spectrum that exists within it. We found the ratings were able to make strong distinctions, though this was facilitated in part by the presence of considerable spreads between organisations regarding impact performance. Analysis was able to identify those organisations that had a clear mission and were operating effectively, thereby producing significant social outcomes which they were able to evidence through engagement with some form of impact measurement and reporting, and typically were transparent, responsive, and so on. And these organisations were reliably distinguished from those that were much less able to articulate what they doing or to demonstrate their impact, and generally exhibited much lower levels of professionalism, alongside greater confusion, less transparency, inadequate planning, and so on. A further relatively simple form of contrast was observed where organisations were pursuing manifestly lower impact activities (sometimes with questions over the extent to which they were truly mission-driven). Given this range of performance the ratings offered a guide to quality, in some ways a little like a star system, as used for example by theatre reviewers (i.e. one star for this show, three stars for that show etc. — and indeed a number of existing impact methodologies do express their results in a star format). By this, the top rating of 1 is more than anything an indication of general excellence, and organisations working in any social-purpose sector are able to achieve a 1 by being outstanding at what they do.

On a practical level, being able to separate out the major groups in terms of impact performance in this way is extremely useful, especially for parties looking to place capital. What this kind of separation does not address however is some of the most challenging intellectual problems that surround the idea of rating impact (and those most frequently put forward when we present the methodology), such as how it is possible to prefer by rating, for example, an excellent employment-focused organisation over an excellent health-focused organisation, or vice versa. Given the spectrum that currently exists regarding impact performance, in which the difference between two excellent organisations will at best be marginal in comparison with the difference with organisations that are at a much less advanced stage regarding how they understand and communicate their impact, such problems simply do not present themselves at the level of a 1-2-3 rating. Were the spectrum to shift and suddenly contain only excellent organisations, the challenge on this front would become much more material (though under such circumstances would be a nice challenge to have). The limited separation the MIAA offers between excellent organisations is also a product of the fact that it is built specifically to allow organisations operating in any sector to score highly, as well as for the cross-sectoral benefits of interventions to be recognised (i.e., using the above example, how better health can lead to improved access to employment, and how employment can engender improved health and well-being). What we felt was important was to ensure that the key things under assessment were that the organisation was effective at delivering its mission, that its activities were bringing meaningful change to beneficiaries, and that these two played into a wider context in a truly impactful way. This responds to the practical realities of what it is useful to be able to distinguish within the contemporary social-purpose universe, but it also relates to what it is pertinent for funders or investors to know. For while the issue of efficacy is likely to be relevant to any party providing capital to social-purpose organisations, questions regarding sectoral direction (such as employment vs. health), are likely to be influenced by a wide range of factors well beyond the reach of the impact analysis of individual organisations.

Capital providers have their own range of concerns, many of which will be exogenous to the analytical concerns of a sector-wide methodology. These may include: the need to balance a portfolio, a mandate to be active in certain sectoral or geographic areas, a particular mission or set of defined policies, and questions of preference. Under such circumstances, and even were it to be possible (though necessarily contentious), it would not be tremendously useful to capital providers at large to have a methodology determining, for example, that this approach to conservation is essentially higher impact than that approach to community finance, but lower impact than this approach to disability care, and so on.[30] What is important is rather to know that this specific social-purpose organisation — whether it runs a conservation scheme, a community finance initiative or a range of disability services — is good at doing what it does, and that what it does is generating real social value. As to the selection among well-run organisations in different high social-value sectors, it will most likely be a point for the capital provider to consider in relation to their own interests and strategy.[31] The role of the analysis is not to make decisions regarding the use of capital, but rather to equip capital providers with the knowledge and understanding needed to be able to use their capital well, and indeed, to invest it for good.

---

30   There are in fact specific cases where there is an explicit desire for precisely this kind of analysis — i.e. one that weighs essentially dissimilar social impacts against each other. For example the National Health Service, in trying to make decisions as to how to allocate funding among different departments and initiatives, may wish to know the comparative impact value on an absolute level between equal financial investments in, say, a smoking prevention campaign and a new mental health programme (assuming both are effectively pursued). Equally local authorities with a limited budget may want to weigh interventions in different sectors on a cost benefit and impact generated basis. However we regard these as specialist applications, and not problems which a general methodology aimed at encompassing the entire social-purpose universe will ever be able to tackle. Indeed the question of whether specialist methodologies in these particular applications are able to tackle problems of this nature is at best open. This is not to say such research is not valuable, only that the results may not be definitive.

31   This in fact is not dissimilar to practices among conventional financial investors, where the financial return of an investment (i.e. the analog to the impact or social return) will certainly always be considered, but is often not the absolute arbiter in decision-making, which will take into account a host of other factors peculiar to a particular investor, such as, again: the need to balance a portfolio, a specific area of interest or expertise, a set of defined policies, a sense of how politics or markets are moving, and questions of preference.

PART II
METHODOLOGY FOR IMPACT ANALYSIS AND ASSESSMENT (MIAA)

0. PREFATORY NOTES

Following the Overview given in Part I, Part II presents the Impact component of the MIAA in full (a complete MIAA analysis comprises also the initial Mapping operation, and the analysis and assessment of Confidence — see above). While the Overview laid out the structure and the core ideas, the following pages unpack these in their actual operational form. The result is essentially a MIAA technical manual.

As with any technical manual, it is, as reading material, somewhat dry. However, while much of the detail can seem abstract on the page, it is thrown into relief in application. When performing an analysis of an organisation, the point by point breakdown of what each part of the analysis is really addressing, and how that aspect of impact can be assessed, suddenly becomes very concrete, and, in an immediately practical way, very handy.

The analysis breaks into three main sections, corresponding to the three key perspectives:

1. Mission Fulfilment
perspective of organisation

2. Beneficiary Perspective
perspective of beneficiaries

3. Wider Impact
perspective of world beyond the organisation and its beneficiaries

Each section starts with a summary table, listing the individual scoring considerations of which it is composed, followed by detailed notes, setting out how these are to be understood and applied. The notes provide a description of what is at stake regarding each consideration, as well as guidelines as to what constitutes an assessment of high, medium or low performance on each. These equip the analyst with stable markers for assigning number-value scores, which is done using the Weighted Impact Scoresheet (see below).

The three main sections are supported by a series of appendices:

4. Appendix A: Weighted Impact Scoresheet

The Weighted Impact Scoresheet collates the considerations from the three analytical sections and accords to each a weight. These weights set the relative significance to the final score. Weighted scores are aggregated to arrive at a total, which in turn is translated into the rating.

5. Appendix B: Impact of Contribution

Impact of Contribution is a bolt-on to the Impact analysis. It acts as a measure of the relative significance of a particular capital contribution to the organisation's activities and overall impact. Impact of Contribution presents an additional analytical section, with a further set of considerations, which similarly are collated into a (smaller) weighted scoresheet. Scores are again totalled, and a separate grade awarded to accompany the Impact rating (see discussion in the Overview above).

6. Appendix C: Beneficiary Perspective Indicator Tables

Analysis of the Beneficiary Perspective (the second of the three main sections) is performed with reference to the set of Indicator Tables. These suggest indicators pertinent to different aspects of the beneficiary-side experience of impact, and serve to support the analyst in their assessment of impact from this perspective.

7. Appendix D: Sample Diagrams

The MIAA supports the presentation of analytical results regarding impact in a number of graphical formats. This section gives a few simple examples.

The MIAA analysis of impact draws on the same essential principles as those set out in the Guidelines for How to Measure and Report Social Impact (presented in Part III). Working with the standard model outlined in Part I, the Guidelines describe a framework for understanding impact measurement and reporting, and the MIAA then places a layer of analysis and assessment on top. Many of the elements in the former lead into specific points for consideration in the latter, and it is therefore useful to read the Guidelines in combination with the MIAA as they provide a full explanation of a number of the core ideas.

1. MISSION FULFILMENT

Mission Fulfilment looks at the organisation's impact in relation to its own stated mission, and its fulfilment thereof. The essential question is: *Is the organisation fulfilling its mission in a meaningful, well-evidenced, and effective fashion?*

The assessment is divided into five sections:

    1.1 Mission Statement
    1.2 Context and Focus
    1.3 Impact Activities
    1.4 Results
    1.5 Moving Forward

The Mission Fulfilment summary table (see overleaf) lays out the considerations that comprise the assessment. These are then worked through one by one over the succeeding pages, which detail how to understand and score each point. The full MIAA Impact Scoresheet is given in 4. Appendix A: Weighted Impact Scoresheet.

1 MISSION FULFILMENT

1.1	**Mission Statement**	
1.1.1	Mission Statement	
	Is the mission statement well-defined and valid in relation to the organisation and its activities? *CHECK FOR: vision, clarity, relevance, in use, reviewed regularly*	
1.2	**Context and Focus**	
1.2.1	Understanding the Problem	
	Does the organisation demonstrate understanding of the wider problem, and use this as the basis for setting the focus and scope of its response? *CHECK FOR: identifying the problem, researching the context, government response, other organisations, broader trends*	
1.2.2	Understanding Beneficiaries	
	Does the organisation demonstrate understanding of its beneficiaries and their needs? *CHECK FOR: identifying beneficiaries, researching and assessing the needs of beneficiaries, understanding the context of beneficiaries, identifying further stakeholders*	
1.3	**Impact Activities**	
1.3.1	Theory of Change	
	Does the organisation's account of its activities, and how these translate into impact through its outputs and outcomes, present a compelling and complete theory of change? *CHECK FOR: coherent and reasonable, defines change for beneficiaries, supported by evidence, other factors acknowledged, clear timeframe, scope*	
1.3.2	Impact Measurement	
	a. Use of Appropriate Indicators Does the organisation use appropriate indicators to measure impact? *CHECK FOR: relevant, responsive, time-bound, specific, consistent, practical*	
	b. Quality of Data Does the organisation gather high quality data? *CHECK FOR: objective, robust, balanced, ongoing*	
	c. Target and Objectives Does the organisation set clear targets and objectives?	
1.3.3	Impact Reporting	
	a. Transparency Does the organisation engage in transparent reporting? *CHECK FOR: regularity, completeness, availability*	
	b. External Validation Does the organisation draw on external sources of validation for its measurement and reporting practices? *CHECK FOR: auditing / use of accredited process (with assurance), use of relevant sector research*	
1.3.4	Balance and Alignment	
	a. Congruence Are the organisation's approach and activities congruent with mission fulfilment? *CHECK FOR: at risk beneficiaries, profitability*	

THE GOOD ANALYST METHODOLOGY FOR IMPACT ANALYSIS AND ASSESSMENT (MIAA)

	b. Attitude to Profit Is the organisation's attitude to profit balanced with its mission?	
	c. Mission Drift Is there a risk of mission drift? *CHECK FOR: liability to mission drift, protection from mission drift*	
1.4	**Results**	
1.4.1	Results	
	a. Delivery of Impact Are the impacts forthcoming in a timely fashion, with capital being used effectively to grow impact?	
	b. Targets and Objectives Is the organisation meeting its targets and objectives (or adapting appropriately)?	
	c. Performance Improvement Is performance improving?	
1.4.2	Accreditation and Comparison	
	a. Accreditation Does the organisation have appropriate external accreditation?	
	b. Class Comparison How does the organisation's performance relate to comparable data and results from other organisations and research?	
1.5	**Moving Forward**	
1.5.1	Results Assessment and Response	
	Does the organisation assess its results, review its operations and systems, and — through feedback processes — respond, make changes, and improve?	
1.5.2	Planning and Strategy	
	Does the organisation have a short term plan and a longer term strategy that show clarity, responsiveness to results, responsiveness to changes in the wider context (including risks and opportunities), and flexibility?	
1.5.3	Sustainability and Growth	
	a. Sustainability of Impacts Are the organisation's projects and impacts self-sustaining and long-lasting?	
	b. Future Growth Is the organisation well positioned to grow, and meet a growing demand or need?	

1.1 Mission Statement

1.1.1 Mission Statement

The mission statement defines the organisation's core aims, and what it hopes to change and achieve. A good mission statement is key to the organisation's coherence and direction. Assessment of the mission statement looks for the following qualities:

vision
The mission statement encapsulates the organisation's vision. It is not simply a summary of what it does nor (in the case of a charity) its legal objects. Instead it looks to the difference the organisation seeks to make, and the purpose of its activities.

clarity
The mission statement clearly establishes the organisation's area of focus and particular approach. It is explicit and specific, giving direction to the organisation as to what it does and does not do.

relevance
The mission statement is valid and meaningful in relation to the organisation's activities, outputs and outcomes. The organisation's impacts tangibly further its stated mission, and the mission guides and informs the medium to long term strategy.

To be effective, the mission statement should be in active use and subject to review:

in use
Staff, volunteers, and trustees are aware of the mission statement and are guided by it. The mission statement is further articulated to funders, investors and the public.

reviewed regularly
The mission statement is reviewed regularly (e.g. annually) to ensure it remains relevant and representative as the organisation develops.

SCORING	
LOW	Mission statement is either not present, or is vague and without direction, and gives little useful guidance to staff or management.
MEDIUM	Mission statement is articulated and relevant, but is incomplete on some of the above qualities, or is not in effective use.
HIGH	Mission statement accords with the above qualities, is in use, and reviewed regularly.

1.2 Context and Focus

The organisation's activities take place within the wider context of the problem it seeks to address. Understanding this problem is critical to ensuring impacts are well-targeted. Equally, understanding the target beneficiaries is critical to ensuring the impacts are an appropriate and desired response. Assessment takes place on these two fronts:

    1.2.1 Understanding the Problem
    1.2.2 Understanding Beneficiaries

1.2.1 Understanding the Problem

Assessment looks to how the organisation demonstrates its understanding of the problem, and how its mission and approach seek to tackle it. Consideration is given to the focus and scope of the organisation's activities, which should be set in the wider context. This context in turn informs strategy.

A well-researched and comprehensive understanding of the problem, forming the basis for a thought-through response, is observed across five fronts:

identifying the problem
The organisation identifies the root problem it seeks to address, and the specific aspects of the problem it focuses on.

researching the context
The organisation demonstrates knowledge of the scale of the problem, its causes, and how it impacts people's lives and the environment. In relation to this the organisation sets the scope for its own work, defining the scale, the area covered, and the magnitude of the impact sought (both in terms of the wider problem and the defined field of activities).

government
The organisation shows awareness of the government response to the problem, including relevant policy, regulations, initiatives etc., as well as government interventions across different relevant scales (national, regional, local). The organisation's activities acknowledge and, where appropriate, engage with local authorities and government.

other organisations
The organisation keeps itself informed of other organisations working with the same problem or similar problems elsewhere, or with the same beneficiaries, with a view to communicating and sharing information, approaches, techniques and results. Where appropriate, partnerships and collaboration are considered. Areas of competition are identified.

broader trends
The organisation considers developments within the sector and in relation to the problem, including the possible influence of new technologies and shifts in public interest, demand, funding, and government. These inform the organisation's assessment of upcoming risks and opportunities.

SCORING	
LOW	There is no evidence of the organisation showing understanding of the problem or the context.
MEDIUM	The organisation has identified the problem and engaged in some research (primary or secondary) in order to inform its response. It shows awareness of its own response and how this plugs into the context.
HIGH	The organisation has researched the problem and formulated its response, both in relation to the local operational level and the wider context. Where appropriate it works with government or other organisations, and keeps itself informed of developments.

1.2.2 Understanding Beneficiaries

Assessment looks to the organisation's understanding of its beneficiaries. This is observed across four fronts:

identifying beneficiaries
Primary beneficiaries are identified (defined by e.g. a particular local area; a section of the public; people with specific support needs; a conservation area, species or the climate; other social-purpose organisations in an umbrella group of some kind).

researching and assessing the needs of beneficiaries
Beneficiary needs are identified, understood, and influence the organisation's response. Researching beneficiary needs may lead to a needs assessment (considered strongest when backed by strategic collection of information e.g. through surveys, questionnaires, discussions with beneficiary groups), which is used to highlight priority needs, and to form a baseline for measuring progress. The monitoring and appraisal of needs is ongoing, and changes in needs are reviewed.

understanding the context of beneficiaries
In addition to beneficiary needs, the contexts of beneficiaries are appraised, with attention paid to particular conditions or circumstances that may affect services to beneficiaries, any other services beneficiaries may be accessing, and any existing or potential resources or assets that may be available.

identifying further stakeholders
Stakeholders beyond the primary beneficiaries — i.e. all those who are materially affected by the organisation and its activities (including e.g. staff, the local community, suppliers, shareholders) — are identified and considered for the impact the organisation has upon them (e.g. wider positive impacts and unintended or negative consequences).

SCORING	
LOW	The organisation identifies its beneficiaries in only a simple or haphazard way, and does not research their needs.
MEDIUM	The organisation knows who it is trying to reach and has made efforts to source their opinion (these however may lack organisation or a clear way to feed into a response).
HIGH	The organisation has well-defined beneficiaries who it consults regularly over their needs (both in relation to the organisation's services and generally), as well as showing awareness of other stakeholders.

1.3 Impact Activities

The impact activities of the organisation are what it does to achieve impact (constituting its theory of change) and how it is evidencing that impact (through its measuring and reporting). These two fields call for consideration also of transparency (of measuring and reporting) and balance and alignment (of operating activities with social or environmental purpose).

These form the four fronts for assessment:

1.3.1 Theory of Change
1.3.2 Impact Measurement
1.3.3 Impact Reporting
1.3.4 Balance and Alignment

1.3.1 Theory of Change

The organisation's theory of change is what connects its operating activities to the generation of positive change for its beneficiaries. This is expressed primarily through the impact chain.

The impact chain starts with a breakdown of activities, mapping what the organisation is doing and what inputs it is using. These activities produce outputs, which in turn lead to outcomes.[1] The impact chain is situated within the context as defined and understood by the organisation (see 1.2 Context and Focus), and serves to confirm the approach, address the identified needs, and further the mission. The impact chain and theory of change implicit within it demonstrate how the organisation's activities as conceived constitute an effective response to the problem.

While an organisation may not use the explicit language of impact chains and theories of change, a compelling and complete picture of how

---

1   Outputs are the immediate results of operating activities (e.g. services supplied, goods distributed); the ensuing outcomes represent the actual social and environmental benefits generated. While outputs focus on things the organisation delivers directly, outcomes speak more of how beneficiaries absorb these into their own lives, and experience change. As such, it is the outcomes that show an organisation's real impact, while the activities and outputs show the mechanics of how it is brought about.

it achieves its impact is an essential component of its impact strategy, and therefore of its ability to achieve impact. Where an overt impact chain and theory of change is not forthcoming, it is expected that information provided by the organisation about its activities and how these translate into impact are sufficient for the analyst to infer the impact chain and theory of change.

Assessment of the theory of change looks for the following qualities:

coherent and reasonable
The links within the impact chain are coherent, as one follows the next with a strong sense of cause and effect, and the outcomes claimed are reasonable in relation to the activities and outputs. In particular, the outcomes are clearly attributable to the related outputs (at least in part if not in full).

defines change for beneficiaries
The impact chain defines the change for beneficiaries, both in terms of the direct benefits delivered, and the ultimate change that the organisation is trying to achieve (these respond to the identified needs, see 1.2 Context and Focus, and key into the mission statement, see 1.1 Mission Statement). The change as defined by the impact chain creates the framework for understanding and measuring progress made toward that change.

supported by evidence
Where possible the theory of change implicit within the impact chain is supported by evidence or examples. These may come from sectoral research, or from the past results of the organisation itself.

other factors acknowledged
Where the outcomes and benefits enjoyed by beneficiaries derive from a number of sources — i.e. the organisation's outputs feature among other factors — these other factors are identified and acknowledged.

clear timeframe
Some outcomes may be readily forthcoming; others may be the long term goal of many years of progress and development (where this is the case it is often useful to identify a "journey of change" and intermediary outcomes or "milestones" along the way — see 1.3.2-a Use of Appropriate Indicators). Outcomes are set within a clear timeframe to help establish: how the chain operates; when different

impacts are expected to be forthcoming; and — where long term outcomes are involved — a case is made for their relationship with the initial impact.

has scope
The organisation's outcomes may present themselves on multiple fronts, and continue spreading and creating new impacts into the future. In drawing up its impact chain the organisation must decide how far to follow these, and to what extent it claims them to be the result of its outputs. The scope of claimed outcomes reflects the scope of the mission and — as these are the outcomes the organisation will need to evidence and track — it sets the scope of the impact measurement system.

SCORING	
LOW	The organisation gives an incomplete account of its activities, and the relationship between its outputs and outcomes is not thought-through.
MEDIUM	The organisation provides a clear map of its activities and how these follow into impact. The movement from outputs to outcomes, though reasoned, may involve assumptions and leave out other factors.
HIGH	The organisation's activities and theory of change are clearly laid out and accord to the above qualities.

1.3.2 Impact Measurement

In order to evidence its impact the organisation must engage in impact measurement. A systematic approach to impact measurement enables the organisation not only to communicate real social and environmental returns to funders and investors, but also to maintain an informed position on what it is genuinely achieving, and to plan and grow accordingly. In this sense the organisation's impact measurement system is seen as an integral part of its impact-generating mechanism. Furthermore, as subsequent layers of the assessment are based on impact information as reported by the organisation, it is important first to analyse and validate the systems producing that information.

Establishing the presence of effective impact measurement is therefore regarded as a vital aspect of the impact assessment.[2] This is observed across three fronts:

a. Use of Appropriate Indicators
b. Quality of Data
c. Targets and Objectives

A. USE OF APPROPRIATE INDICATORS

Indicators are the specific variables used to track key elements within the impact chain. Information from these indicators is then used to build a tangible, meaningful, and evidenced picture of the benefits achieved.

Effective impact measurement systems use a number of indicators, or an "indicator set", which taken as a whole tracks information about both outputs and outcomes. The precise indicator set of any organisation will depend upon the particular focus of its mission, as well as its scale and resourcing capacity. This assessment methodology strongly believes that organisations themselves, with their unique knowledge of their own activities and beneficiaries, are best positioned to select the most appropriate indicators for measuring their own impact.

The key quality for an indicator set is that it addresses the things that are most important to the organisation and its beneficiaries — i.e. the indicator set is used to demonstrate the impacts that really matter.

Organisations working with long term projects may not be able to measure and demonstrate final outcomes on a year-on-year basis. In such cases it is useful to consider what stages or "milestones" are passed on the way toward

---

2 The measurement and reporting of impact among different organisations will inevitably vary in terms of depth and character, and be influenced by a host of different factors, including the level of experience an organisation has with impact measurement, and the volume of resources it devotes to it. Smaller organisations may find some of the more sophisticated points of measurement to be less relevant to their operations; younger organisations will naturally have less by way of track record to illustrate what they do. Conversely, while larger, more mature organisations may have more capacity for producing attractive-looking documents, they may not be able to achieve the same level of direct detail in their reporting across a number of different centres and activities. Assessment of an organisation's impact measurement must therefore be sensitive to the size of the organisation, comparing its reporting to a sense of what would be appropriate (for this — as in other areas of the analysis — the analyst may look to comparison with of peers of different kinds, including comparisons with respect to sector, size, stage of development and geographic area). The Guidelines for How to Measure and Report Social Impact given in Part III lay out a comprehensive vocabulary of parts for good impact measurement and reporting, as well as indicating which parts are considered essential, and which more elaborate, and potentially esoteric.

the final outcomes, where progress may become visible, as well as what intermediary outcomes contributing to progress have been achieved. This is sometimes referred to as a "journey of change". Formulating a journey of change for beneficiaries allows the organisation to find indicators for specific points along the journey.

For organisations in other fields, maintaining a situation from year to year (i.e. no change) may in fact be a key outcome, and represent an important impact. Here indicators that demonstrate stability are applicable.

The purpose of indicators and impact measurement is not to produce a large number or high ratio, but to identify what — given the organisation's mission and approach — it hopes to achieve over a reporting period, and to apply indicators that can tell whether or not this has happened.

Assessment of the Use of Appropriate Indicators looks for the following qualities:

relevant
The indicators are relevant to the organisation's goals and indicative of the real benefits outlined in the mission statement.

responsive
The indicators are sensitive to change (i.e. an indicator which always gives the result "3" is not useful).

time-bound
The indicators fluctuate over time with the element being tracked, and do so within the reporting period (i.e. to provide new readings at least from one year to the next).

specific
The indicators are specific as to what is being measured and exist on a well-defined scale, such that the measurement can be taken again in the same way (e.g. for the next reporting period) and against the same scale (on which e.g. a "3" will mean the same thing).

consistent
The indicators perform consistently (i.e. repeat measurements give the same result), forming a reliable basis for comparison (the primary requirement is to be able to compare results from one reporting period to the next).

practical
The indicators are simple and relatively quick and cheap to use, making them practical and realistic for taking regular measurements (at least once a year).

SCORING	
LOW	Indicators are either not used, or are isolated and track only outputs.
MEDIUM	The organisation follows outputs and possibly some outcomes, though lacks a complete system for tracking impact.
HIGH	Indicators form a coherent set and accord with the above qualities.

B. QUALITY OF DATA

Beyond selecting appropriate indicators, the organisation must implement their use into its operations in order to gather high quality data. Almost invariably, data collection which is planned and systematic produces more accurate and more cost-effective results.

The organisation's account of how it captures data must demonstrate a credible and reliable process. Assessment of the quality of the data looks for the following:

objective
Data collection techniques are objective, and the results produced give a reasonably complete picture (i.e. relevant data is not omitted, and results are in keeping with the realities of outcomes). Underlying assumptions are clearly laid out and where necessary supported (these may relate to the treatment of samples or proxies, or any important background information used to build an understanding of impact, or for calculations with results).

robust
The data is robust (i.e. accurate, consistent, specific etc.). This may include consideration of double-counting (e.g. a beneficiary showing up multiple times using the same service), and of the margin of error in the data.

balanced
The data is able to capture both good and bad performance. This is essential to facilitate a balanced assessment, and for identifying areas for learning and improvement. Organisations which are able to

spot weaknesses in performance and adapt are far more convincing models of efficiency than those which are unaware of how well or badly they are doing.

ongoing
The data measurement systems are set up for ongoing monitoring into the future. Where possible future results are designed to be comparable with previous results (and so use the same or equivalent indicators). If a change in focus or activities prevents this, appropriate steps are taken to provide a basis for ongoing comparison.

SCORING	
LOW	The organisation's data is patchy, and includes no account of how it has been collected.
MEDIUM	The organisation has good data on preferred measures, though this possibly leaves some questions.
HIGH	The organisation presents high quality data, including the method of collection, an accounting for error, and inclusion of performance shortcomings.

C. TARGETS AND OBJECTIVES

Targets and objectives relate to the specific indicators used to track outputs and outcomes. Not all targets and objectives need to be numerical quantities (e.g. x beneficiaries receiving services, x products delivered), but they do need to provide a usable baseline against which to measure results, such that the questions: 'Has the organisation carried out its plan as intended?' and 'Has it been successful?' can be meaningfully addressed.

Assessment looks for the use of targets and objectives by the organisation, with ideally a target for each key output and an objective (or beneficiary aim) for each key outcome within the impact chain. These serve to set clear goals, which themselves relate to the core aims of the mission.

SCORING	
LOW	No targets and objectives.
MEDIUM	The organisation has targets and objectives for some things, but these are incomplete, and potentially arbitrarily set.
HIGH	Targets and objectives with meaningfully set levels.

1.3.3 Impact Reporting

Subsequent to impact measurement, impact reporting is the process by which the organisation makes its results public. Assessment of impact reporting takes place across two fronts:

    a. Transparency
    b. External Validation

A. TRANSPARENCY
Transparency is a measure of the extent to which an organisation's reporting gives a comprehensive and faithful overall picture of the organisation's activities, achievements, and shortcomings. Looking at the reporting provided, an analyst should be able to say whether or not an organisation is effective in its mission fulfilment. Assessment looks for the following qualities:

> **regular impact reporting**
> All organisations must report on their impact. This may take the form of a social or environmental report, or the inclusion of substantial social or environmental reporting within the annual report. It may be further supported by more frequent reporting of results e.g. through newsletters. Assessment is sensitive to the scale of the organisation, acknowledging that extensive reporting presents significant costs, and elaborate printed documents are feasible only for larger organisations. However irrespective of size, the regular publication of current information on impact (including online-only formats) is at the core of transparency.

> **completeness**
> The reporting supplies the core information necessary to gain a realistic overview of the organisation's activities and impact. This covers the organisation's mission and theory of change, and the presentation of results that are valid, complete and consistent (i.e. are in accord with the principles of impact measurement as laid out above, including objectivity, balance etc.).

availability
Information on the organisation's impact is readily available (e.g. through the organisation's website, preferably within a few clicks of the homepage).

SCORING	
LOW	Little to no impact reporting forthcoming.
MEDIUM	The organisation reports on impact, but these reports are possibly incomplete, late and hard to access.
HIGH	The organisation engages in regular transparent impact reporting.

B. EXTERNAL VALIDATION

Assessment of the validation of the organisation's systems for impact measurement and reporting relates to the extent to which these take account of external research in the field, and use it to enhance the quality of impact reporting.

Formal external validation of impact reporting can take the form of a third party auditing of results, or the results may be compiled using an accredited process, with the final report being assured (i.e. "stamped" by the relevant assurance body). However external auditing or accreditation can be an expensive process, and should be considered in relation to the scale of the organisation and its available resources.

Without seeking formal external validation, the organisation may nevertheless have researched guidelines, toolkits and best practice manuals from relevant sector bodies, and have developed its approach with this information in mind. The organisation may also have looked to the impact reporting of other similar organisations to consider what techniques and indicators are currently in use elsewhere.

Assessment looks to the organisation's use of external verification, sources, and relevant sector learning in developing a mature impact measurement and reporting system.

SCORING	
LOW	The organisation shows no awareness of external developments in impact reporting.
MEDIUM	The organisation has researched impact measurement and formed its own systems in response.
HIGH	The organisation has clear external validation of its methods or results.

1.3.4 Balance and Alignment

The issue of Balance and Alignment addresses the relationship between on the one hand the organisation's impact-generating activities, and on the other its financial stability and, in the case of for-profit social enterprises, profitability. For-profit aspects of the organisation must exhibit mission-alignment; impact-generating activities must balance with financial viability.

Assessment takes place across three fronts:

    a. Congruence
    b. Attitude to Profit
    c. Mission Drift

A. CONGRUENCE
Congruence scrutinises the relationship between benefit generation and revenue generation. The operational approach of the organisation should ensure the two are yoked together, with the model for perfect congruence being one where mission-fulfilment drives financial success and vice versa.

However it may be that, within the bounds of a certain level of mission fulfilment, a balance is struck between delivering impact and maintaining financial stability, with payoff and compromise on either side. The management of this balance is observed in relation to at risk beneficiaries, and profitability.

i. At Risk Beneficiaries
The organisation may find a conflict exists between serving the most at risk beneficiaries and the operational interests of the organisation. Higher risk beneficiaries may be more demanding of resources and result in slower turnarounds (for organisations geared toward supplying services), and they may also present higher risks financially (e.g. for lending organisations). However these beneficiaries may also be the most excluded or underserved, and therefore those who stand to benefit most from the organisation's work. For example a social enterprise focused on employment may find there is an operational incentive to select those beneficiaries who are more capable, but in so doing, neglect those who are most in need.

Assessment on this front looks to the extent to which the organisation's focus and activities are exposed to this conflict of at risk beneficiaries presenting at once higher impacts and potentially compromised operational viability. Lower exposure (i.e. there is little or no operational incentive to select out less vulnerable beneficiaries) equates to greater congruence.

ii. Profitability
For organisations whose operating income is derived from its beneficiaries there may be a strain between profitability and beneficiary affordability. This can be particularly pronounced with organisations whose target beneficiaries are the poor, as maintaining a profit margin implies transferring a greater burden of cost to those with the least resources to deal with it. Microfinance provides a clear example, where very low lending rates are favourable to borrowers, but are likely to bring about the collapse of the microfinance institution; conversely, higher lending rates are favourable to the microfinance institution, but may draw borrowers into cycles of debt rather than help them progress out of poverty. Trading organisations focused on groups that are financially disadvantaged are likely to have to strike a balance between the financial interests of the group and those of the business. It is crucial that the relationship between the organisation and its target beneficiaries is equitable not exploitative, and that business practices are productive (wealth-generating within the group) not extractive (drawing off wealth or labour from the group).

Assessment on this front looks to the extent to which there is a potential strain between the mission and profit margin, with greater levels of strain equating to lower congruence.

SCORING	
LOW	The organisation's approach presents considerable threats to congruence from either at risk beneficiaries or profit-margin interests, with reasonable concern that these are compromising impact.
MEDIUM	The organisation's approach presents potential concerns over congruence, though these are directly addressed by the organisation.
HIGH	There is no issue over congruence.

B. ATTITUDE TO PROFIT
Attitude to Profit assessment looks to the organisation's expressed attitude to profit, and that borne out by its behaviour. (This is applicable primarily to organisations formed as for-profit enterprises; not-for-profit organisations

that are unable to extract profits from operations are less likely to face challenges over their attitude to profit.) This is distinct from the previous address of Profitability under Congruence (see above), in that while Profitability looked to the theoretical strain implied by the organisation's approach, Attitude to Profit considers the actual attitudes displayed.

The organisation's attitude to profit is reflected in its operating margins (focusing on the question of whether or not the organisation is geared toward maximisation), and also in its use of operating profits. The use of profits may similarly suggest a weighting of interest within the organisation, with the chief groups competing for company profits most likely being investors, the organisation itself (in the sense of growth-orientated reinvestment), and target beneficiaries (organisations may use profits to run mission-related philanthropic schemes, e.g. providing free education or healthcare to beneficiaries).

Organisations that are strongly orientated toward generating high investor returns may appear less mission-focused. However the level of financial return will also reflect the profitability of the sector (e.g. clean technology companies are more likely to be able to offer high returns), as well as the organisation's sense of its own risk-return profile, and the structure of its investment proposition. For example, in order to attract capital, an organisation may offer higher return tranches of debt supported by philanthropic funds. Here the higher return offer does not reflect a mission-threatening attitude to profit on the part of the organisation, but rather is part of a capital-raising strategy.

High investor returns which do not exert a strain upon the mission, and do promote the capital raising interests of the organisation as well as incentivising performance, may equally be high impact. However, organisations which distribute profits to investors when the interests of mission-furtherment would be more toward reinvestment, charitable schemes, or smaller profit margins, are considered lower impact with respect to their attitude to profit.

The income of the organisation's top management may also be a relevant consideration. Income should be proportional both to the skill and commitment of the top management, as well as to the performance of the organisation.

The alignment of the organisation's attitude to profit with its mission, and the balance between different groups in the distribution of profits, is assessed, with better aligned attitudes and more impact-weighted balances equating to a higher impact attitude to profit.

SCORING	
LOW	The organisation's attitude to profit is cutting into impact.
MEDIUM	The organisation has clear profit interests which it balances with its impact.
HIGH	There are no issues or concerns regarding profit.

C. MISSION DRIFT

Mission drift describes the process by which an organisation gradually loses touch with its core mission. Assessment focuses on two fronts:

i. Liability to Mission Drift

Liability to mission drift looks to the potential for an organisation to move further away from impact and more toward business interests. This is distinct from the Congruence consideration of At Risk Beneficiaries (see 1.3.4-a above), which looked to the theoretical case for an organisation to "cherry-pick" less at risk beneficiaries, in that Liability to Mission Drift looks to the theoretical case for an organisation to shift its activities, focus (including potentially its target beneficiaries), and business model.

Liability to mission drift is likely to be sensitive to the sector and operating activities of the organisation, which may or may not present a path toward faster growth at the cost of mission fulfilment. Organisations whose core business does not present an opportunity for mission drift are considered less liable, and therefore are assessed to be better aligned on this measure.

ii. Protection from Mission Drift

Organisations may incorporate into their company structure or constitutions provisions to protect the organisation from mission drift. The organisation's mission statement and the presence of a board of directors or trustees overseeing the organisation's operations may form part of a strategy to ensure that practices remain well-aligned to the core mission. In addition to this oversight, it is important the mission itself is regularly reviewed for balance and alignment with what the organisation is actually doing. Additional measures to protect against mission drift may include formal rules regarding operating practices.

Assessment looks for evidence of protection from mission drift in the organisation's constitution, in its structure and managerial processes, and in its formal operating procedures.

SCORING	
LOW	The organisation presents a clear and unaddressed risk of mission drift.
MEDIUM	The organisation presents a risk of mission drift, though this is mitigated by formal measures.
HIGH	The organisation is not at risk of mission drift.

1.4 Results

Following the assessment of the quality of the impact measurement and reporting is the assessment of the actual results achieved. While the focus of 1.3 Impact Activities was on the organisation's approach and systems (its theory of change, its means to measure that change or impact, and its operational model), 1.4 Results turns to the real impacts as delivered and evidenced through the application of that approach, and by the use of those systems.

Assessment is made of the organisation's results over the reporting period on two fronts:

    1.4.1 Results
    1.4.2 Accreditation and Comparison

1.4.1 Results

Assessment of Results looks for clear evidence of impact generated over the reporting period (itself clearly defined). The results must cover the organisation's key events and achievements, as well as any improvements introduced or new products or services offered, and any other significant changes.

At the core of the presentation of results is the data from indicator measurements, demonstrating the outputs and outcomes delivered over the reporting period (in line with the organisation's theory of change). Assessment then looks for the timely delivery of impact, and compares results with the organisation's targets and objectives (as set at the start of the reporting period), and against performance over previous reporting periods. These form the three assessment fronts:

    a. Delivery of Impact
    b. Targets and Objectives
    c. Performance Improvement

A. DELIVERY OF IMPACT

Assessment of the Delivery of Impact looks to whether the progression from activities through to outputs, outcomes and ultimately impact is indeed occurring, and in a timely fashion. Organisations engaged in activities and with beneficiaries where long periods — or lead times — are anticipated between the intervention and the impact are not to be penalised for this, though they are expected to have formulated a journey of change, with milestones along the way by which progress can be measured and evidenced within the reporting period (see 1.3.2-a Use of Appropriate Indicators).

Delivery of Impact looks to whether results indicate the organisation is actively realising impact according to the path and timeline laid out by its impact chain and theory of change.

An important aspect of this is to look specifically at the organisation's inputs (e.g. investment capital, funding) and expenditure over the reporting period, and consider the extent to which these are following through into the measured outputs and impact. Increased inputs, organisational growth and boosted impact must all be strongly positively correlated, with results that demonstrate how capital in is resulting in impact growth. Socially-motivated capital providers can only sensibly engage with an organisation if there is a clear line between investing new capital and the increased generation of positive outcomes.

Organisations are assessed for the extent to which they use capital to grow impact in a proportional and effective fashion. A simple manifestation of this may involve new capital being channelled directly into expanding output-generating activities (as tracked by effective indicators). Investments in indirect growth operations, such as for example expenditures on marketing or office costs, may equally be impact building, but a greater burden of proof lies with the organisation to demonstrate the link between the investment and increased impact. Assessment looks for a strong and efficient relationship between the inputs used and the impact achieved.

A further aspect of this is to consider unused inputs or underexploited potential resources. Most obviously this looks to the extent to which the organisation is mobilising its investable capital. High proportions of actively invested capital (i.e. funds deployed in operational activities) represent an ambitious gearing toward the generation of impacts. On the other hand, a lack of deal-flow, bottlenecks or other complications may result in funds not being disbursed into impact-generating activities (and typically held instead as cash, or invested in commercial liquid assets to generate a return while waiting to be used). It is clearly important for organisations to maintain adequate reserves, but large volumes of inactive capital (inactive with respect to impact) suggest a weakness in this regard.

Assessment of Delivery of Impact looks for the presence of results that convincingly evidence both the generation of impact, and the correlation between that impact and the organisation's use of capital.

SCORING	
LOW	Impacts are not forthcoming, and growth in the organisation's balance sheet or inputs results in little change.
MEDIUM	Impacts are forthcoming, but possibly in a compromised form or incompletely evidenced. Organisational growth and growth in impact follow one another, though the linkage is potentially obscure, and new capital does not clearly leverage high levels of new impact. An appreciable volume of capital is not being used for impact-related activities.
HIGH	Impacts are forthcoming and fully evidenced, with the use of capital clearly driving impact in an effective, committed, and — with reference to new capital — scalable way.

B. TARGETS AND OBJECTIVES

Where 1.3.2-c Targets and Objectives looked for the presence of targets and objectives in the organisations's impact measurement systems, 1.4.1-b looks to the meeting of those targets and objectives in the organisation's results. Performance against targets and objectives can form a useful baseline for gauging if the envisioned progress has been made. However, it is important to review performance against targets and objectives in a nuanced fashion rather than using a straight hit / miss approach (which can be manipulated simply by low target-setting). The review seeks to unpack the organisation's performance, taking into consideration things which emerged during the reporting period that affected results. This covers external factors (e.g. changes in government programmes or policies, changes in the local environment or context) and internal changes (e.g. changes in funding, available inputs, strategy). Assessment is of whether or not the organisation's results show it has been performing effectively over the reporting period as it developed — either delivering upon its target and objectives, or adapting appropriately.

SCORING	
LOW	The organisation is failing to meet its targets and objectives without being able to explain why.
MEDIUM	The organisation is performing satisfactorily against its targets and objectives as viewed in relation to developments over the reporting period.

INVESTING FOR GOOD

| HIGH | The organisation is successfully meeting or exceeding its targets and objectives and is performing well in relation to developments over the period. |

C. PERFORMANCE IMPROVEMENT

Assessment compares results for this reporting period with those of the previous and looks for evidence of improvement. This may show as growth in volumes of outputs and outcomes, as well as an expanded range of outputs and outcomes (e.g. through new services and products). Together these demonstrate the organisation is achieving year on year progress in its impact.

Benchmarks may be used to strengthen the case for performance improvement. The consistent use of a valid measurement system will furnish the organisation with comparable results on a year-on-year basis. This allows benchmarks to be set that are sensitive to the organisation's particular approach, and illustrate tangibly the development of impact through time.

SCORING	
LOW	The organisation is not able to demonstrate improved performance.
MEDIUM	The organisation's performance is improving moderately.
HIGH	The organisation is able to show high levels of performance improvement following from previous reporting periods into the current.

1.4.2 Accreditation and Comparison

Assessment of Accreditation and Comparison looks at the organisation's results in the context of its sector other relevant bodies and organisations. Assessment takes place on two fronts:

   a. Accreditation
   b. Class Comparison

A. ACCREDITATION

Assessment considers any accreditation the organisation may have (or lack) from external bodies regarding its operations and activities (as opposed to for its impact reporting, as in 1.3.3-b). Accreditation of this kind may cover, among other things: the organisation itself (e.g. CDFIs); the organisation's suppliers (e.g. fairtrade producers supplying fairtrade retailers); the organisation's products (e.g. BREEAM certified green buildings built by a green property development company); enterprises in which the organisation invests (e.g. environmental companies producing certified carbon credits); the organisation's own processes (e.g. ISO14001).

Assessment looks to the extent to which the organisation has made use of appropriate external accreditation, and, to a lesser degree, the extent to which the sector in which the organisation is operating is accredited. An organisation working in a sector with little available accreditation or external information will inevitably be less well accredited. Weaker however is an organisation working in a sector where appropriate accreditation is available and yet has not been sought or achieved.

SCORING	
LOW	The organisation lacks clearly relevant and available accreditation.
MEDIUM	The organisation has looked to accreditation but is either yet to receive it, or is operating in an field in which little relevant accreditation exists.
HIGH	The organisation is appropriately accredited.

B. CLASS COMPARISON

Class Comparison looks to the organisation's impact-generating performance in relation to comparable data and results from other organisations and findings from relevant research. This may include comparison with the performance of other similar and possibly competing organisations, but also comparison with past data, data from elsewhere, or data from different approaches to similar problems. All of these may be used to throw the organisation's results into relief against the wider sector, and substantiate their validity.

Comparison looks where possible for the use of benchmarks. Benchmarks for the specific indicators the organisation is reporting on may not be immediately forthcoming, or not applicable to the particular approach in use. As impact reporting matures, it is likely benchmarks will become increasingly prevalent, and information about benchmarks common to particular sectors will become more available.

Further areas for Class Comparison may be furnished via the mapping operations (see discussion in Part I, 3. MIAA: Development and Overview). While direct equivalents among mission-driven organisations are rare, and social impact takes a wide variety of different forms, the mapped profile provides the analyst with grounds to create classes of organisations based on commonality of specific attributes. The most appropriate organisations for comparison may be different for different areas, forming multiple classes of peers (e.g. scale, sector, stage of development). The assessment of Class Comparison takes a balanced overview of the organisation's results on the measures listed above (i.e. 1.4.1-a Delivery of Impact, 1.4.1-b Targets and Objectives, 1.4.1-c Performance Improvement) against relevant performance elsewhere.

SCORING	
LOW	The organisation does not engage in class comparison or benchmarking itself, and when looked at against the performance of other organisations appears weak.
MEDIUM	The organisation appears to be performing reasonably within its class (though lack of comparable data may make it difficult to establish further than that).
HIGH	The organisation shows excellent performance when compared with others in its class, as demonstrated through the use of comparable data and where possible benchmarks.

1.5 Moving Forward

Moving Forward considers the organisation's response to its results, and its strategy for the future.
Assessment takes place on three fronts:

1.5.1 Results Assessment and Response
1.5.2 Planning and Strategy
1.5.3 Sustainability and Growth

1.5.1 Results Assessment and Response

The power of impact measurement is that it provides the organisation with essential information for learning and improving going into the future. Consequently it is crucial for the organisation to address the questions:

- what can we learn from our results and experience?
- how can we respond?

Assessment looks for evidence that results and past performance are being assessed, and that appropriate lessons are being drawn. This includes addressing activities and identifying which are working well and which less well, as well as a consideration of efficiency regarding resources. Conclusions can then feed into a general review of operations (including a review of governing documents and organisational policies and procedures), and lead to the formulation of appropriate responses and improvements. Assessment looks in particular to the organisation's ability to make changes according to what its results show.

As impact results can play a powerful role in managerial decision-making in this regard, it is important also to review the impact measurement systems, and ensure that the results capture the impacts in a coherent and balanced fashion (as well as that the measurement processes are themselves practical, streamlined, accurate etc.). On this front, it may be useful for the organisation to consider the responses to results from the people working with them — i.e. frontline staff and beneficiaries — who can offer valuable insights regarding which activities and outcomes they felt were most successful and valuable. Reviewing results in this way can help verify the quality of the results, and reflect thereby on the measurement system being used to produce them.

SCORING	
LOW	The organisation shows little or no signs of assessing its own results or reviewing its operations.
MEDIUM	The organisation engages in results assessment and identifies key things that have influenced results over the period, though is less clear about how to act in response. Some aspects of policies and operations are reviewed, though not others.
HIGH	The organisation's results assessment shows clearly the relative successes of different activities which, supported by comprehensive and effective reviewing (including a review of the quality of the results themselves), enables the organisation to respond appropriately, make changes, and improve.

1.5.2 Planning and Strategy

Assessment looks to the organisation's planning and strategy for the future. It is important that plans incorporate the response from the results assessment (see above), but further to this, that they key this response into the wider context and developments taking place beyond their own immediate operations (see 1.2 Context and Focus, especially the point of broader trends within 1.2.1 Understanding the Problem). These may include:

- changes in policy or regulations
- changes in demand or funding
- new technologies
- changing needs among beneficiaries.

By assessing ongoing changes to its context the organisation is able to inform its understanding of upcoming risks and opportunities, and plan accordingly.

Assessment looks for a short term plan (e.g. 1 year) that is well-defined, takes account of results and any upcoming changes in the context, and has a clear path to implementation. The plan includes the setting of targets and objectives for the next reporting period, and, if there are significant shifts in activities, these follow through into an updated impact chain and theory of change, with appropriate indicators to measure success going into the future. The strategy (e.g. 3–5 years) addresses ongoing trends over the longer term, and establishes the larger framework for the organisation's continuing mission fulfilment.

Together the planning and strategy express a strong position moving forward, and cover:

- the identification of risks, and measures to mitigate them
- the identification of new opportunities or needs arising from the changing context, and ideas for how to respond
- a clear focus of energy on the areas most effective for mission fulfilment

An important aspect of the organisation, with regard to planning and strategy, is that it is, where appropriate, flexible. This includes the ability to adapt and innovate — i.e. try new things — as well as being willing to close existing projects that are underperforming or no longer relevant.

SCORING	
LOW	The organisation has only basic or ill-defined plans and limited longer term strategy. It shows little awareness of any upcoming (potential) changes in the context, and little interest in making changes itself.
MEDIUM	The organisation engages in planning and strategy, though it is perhaps not clear how these will be carried out, or how they may be affected by wider changes. The planning and strategy suggest some flexibility, though there is limited history of flexibility.
HIGH	The organisation has an effective short term plan and processes to implement it, and a long term strategy in place. These respond appositely to the results assessment and to an understanding of upcoming risks and opportunities. The organisation has a history of flexibility, and this is borne out in the plan for the future.

1.5.3 Sustainability and Growth

Sustainability and Growth looks to the sustainability of the organisation's impacts and its potential for future growth.

Assessment takes place on two fronts:

a. Sustainability of Impacts
b. Future Growth

A. SUSTAINABILITY OF IMPACTS

Assessment considers the sustainability of projects with regard to their own ability to continue generating impacts, and the longevity of the impacts themselves.

Projects and outcomes are considered least sustainable if they have an obvious finite lifetime, more sustainable if they have a continued existence but only with continued intervention, and most sustainable if they envisage a fully self-sustaining existence outside of the organisation.

SCORING	
LOW	The impacts have a finite lifetime.
MEDIUM	The impacts are sustainable with continued intervention.
HIGH	The impacts are self-sustaining.

B. FUTURE GROWTH

Assessment of Future Growth considers the organisation's prospects for growth (and thereby for impact growth) on the two fronts of market growth or need, and organisation growth.

i. Market Growth or Need

This refers to the demand for the organisation's products or services, and relates to both the sector and geography of operations. It looks to the extent to which the organisation is focused on a particular problem or issue that presents a growing — or large yet underaddressed — need, and therefore the potential for a substantial rise in demand for the social or environmental services or products it offers. The key factors when considering market growth or need are:

- the current market size (i.e. the current number of service or product users)
- the size of the addressable market (i.e. the number of potential service or product users)

- the readiness of the addressable market (i.e. the extent to which the addressable market is ready to create new demand for services or products)
- recent history of growth

Market growth or need is assessed to be strongest when the current market has some size and history of growth, and yet is small relative to the greater need.

ii. Organisation Growth

This addresses the organisation's own prospects for growth. On a direct operational level this looks to the scalability of operations and evidence of new deal flow, as well as the organisation's access to growth capital and unrestricted funds, and past growth performance. Also considered is the ambition of the organisation, interpreted in relation to its approach, planning and strategy, and its plans for future capital-raising. Assessment looks to prospects for feasible and well-resourced growth.

SCORING	
LOW	The organisation shows limited signs of growth and operates in a sector or area where there is little market growth or need.
MEDIUM	The organisation shows some signs of growth, though this is potentially limited by the scalability of its operations, its access to capital, and the extent of the demand.
HIGH	The organisation shows strong signs of growth to meet a clearly growing — or large but underaddressed — need for its services or products.

2. BENEFICIARY PERSPECTIVE

Beneficiary Perspective considers the organisation and its impact with respect to the beneficiary perspective. The essential question is: *What is the value to your beneficiaries of the impact you are generating?*

Analysis of the beneficiary perspective is a compelling way to help establish that an organisation works with its beneficiaries, and empowers them wherever possible to achieve their own personal goals. It ensures that the progress of beneficiaries, rather than the development of the organisation itself, remains at the heart of operations.

For organisations working with beneficiaries who are themselves less able to express their views directly, an important aspect of understanding the beneficiary perspective can be to engage with family members, carers, or others who are able to contribute on their behalf. This may relate to how such organisations are able to incorporate beneficiary input into their planning and services.

Assessment is divided into two sections: Beneficiary Focus, which considers the beneficiary's relationship with the organisation, and Beneficiary Impacts, which considers the nature of the impact upon beneficiaries' lives.

2.1 Beneficiary Focus
2.2 Beneficiary Impacts

The Beneficiary Perspective summary table (see overleaf) lays out the considerations that comprise the assessment. These are then worked through over the succeeding pages, which detail how to understand and score them one by one.

In addition to this detailing, the analysis of each consideration is supported by an indicator table. These tables set out the principle areas of focus, key points and potential indicators that may be used to express and evidence impact in those areas. The tables are not aimed to be exhaustive (a complete listing of all the different kinds of impacts an organisation may achieve and the indicators it may use to track them would be neither feasible nor desirable within a methodology); nor do they present a checklist of the impacts an organisation must be achieving and indicators it must be using to score on a particular consideration. Instead they offer a research and analysis reference point. They provide the analyst with a broad set of criteria relating to each consideration which, taken together, outline what is typically at stake when looking at a specific area of impact, and what kinds of benefits are frequently observed. In particular, with the Matrix of Human, Social and Environmental Rights and Benefits, which constitutes the analysis in section 2.2.1, and which treats the various fields of social-purpose action, the indicator tables work to ground the analyst within those fields, and provide a framework by which to gauge the impacts being reported by the organisation. The points and potential indicators within each table help define what exactly the consideration encompasses, and can serve to highlight and ratify certain positive outcomes the organisation is achieving, as well as suggesting areas where it is missing an important element or failing to keep up with best practice. If an organisation is generating an impact which is completely new, its newness, and its value in relation to more standard approaches, can equally be shown up through use of the tables.

The indicator tables are to be used for reference when performing an analysis, and are set out in 6. Appendix C: Beneficiary Perspective Indicator Tables.

The full MIAA Impact Scoresheet (including Beneficiary Perspective) is set out in 4. Appendix A: Weighted Impact Scoresheet.

2 BENEFICIARY PERSPECTIVE

2.1 Beneficiary Focus

2.1.1 Beneficiary Awareness, Access and Inclusion

Are beneficiaries aware of the organisation and the support it provides? Can beneficiaries access the support? Is the organisation's outreach inclusive, representative and diverse?

2.1.2 Beneficiary Consultation

Are beneficiaries being consulted?

2.1.3 Beneficiary Empowerment

Are beneficiaries being empowered by the organisation to achieve their own personal goals?
CHECK FOR: participation in activities, use of capital, defining impact, role with organisation

2.1.4 Beneficiaries Connect

Are beneficiaries being supported to communicate and develop social networks?

2.1.5 Beneficiary Satisfaction

Is there evidence of beneficiary satisfaction with the organisation's impact?

2.2 Beneficiary Impacts

2.2.1 Matrix of Human, Social and Environmental Rights and Benefits
What is the depth of change?

    a. Education and Family
       Impacts advance beneficiary access to the right to education and the right to enjoy family life in a safe and supportive environment.

    b. Employment
       Impacts advance beneficiary access to the right to employment.

    c. Housing and Essential Needs
       Impacts advance beneficiary access to the right to housing within a healthy and sustainable environment, and the right to adequate provisions regarding domestic and home needs.

    d. Economic Factors
       Impacts advance beneficiary access to rights to economic means and security.

    e. Health
       Impacts advance beneficiary access to the right to the highest attainable standard of physical and mental health.

    f. High Risk Behaviour
       Impacts help beneficiaries manage high risk behaviour.

    g. Care of Disabled and Older People
       Impacts advance the access of disabled and older people to the right to a healthy and fulfilling life and the right to be as independently capable as possible.

    h. Safety and Community
       Impacts advance beneficiary access to the right to a sense of community, and the right to personal safety and freedom from discrimination.

	i. Arts, Culture and Sports Impacts advance beneficiary access to the right to participation in cultural life including arts and sports.	
	j. Information, Understanding and Expression Impacts advance beneficiary access to information and understanding regarding the issues under address, and access to the right to expression.	
	k. Local Environment Impacts advance beneficiary access to the right to live in a healthy and sustainable local environment with adequate infrastructure and community space.	
	l. Well-Being Impacts advance the right to well-being.	
	m. Conservation and Biodiversity Impacts advance the conservation of natural and cultural heritage, natural ecosystems, and biodiversity.	
	n. Greenhouse Gas Emissions Impacts serve to reduce global greenhouse gas emissions.	
	o. Consumption, Waste, Pollution and Recycling Impacts safeguard natural resources and promote environmentally responsible practices	
2.2.2	Unit Cost	
	What is the breadth of change? *CHECK FOR: accuracy and transparency, efficiency within sector, overall breadth*	

2.1 Beneficiary Focus

Beneficiary Focus considers the relationship between the beneficiary and the organisation. Analysis focuses on ways in which the beneficiary perspective is included in processes and contributes to the direction and development of the organisation.

Assessment takes place across five fronts:

   2.1.1 Beneficiary Awareness, Access and Inclusion
   2.1.2 Beneficiary Consultation
   2.1.3 Beneficiary Empowerment
   2.1.4 Beneficiaries Connect
   2.1.5 Beneficiary Satisfaction

Assessment on each is supported by and performed with reference to the indicator tables, located in 6. Appendix C: Beneficiary Perspective Indicator Tables.

2.1.1 Beneficiary Awareness, Access and Inclusion

Beneficiary Awareness, Access and Inclusion considers whether those among the organisation's population of target beneficiaries are aware of and have access to the organisation's services. Consideration is also given to whether the organisation's outreach is inclusive with respect to its mission and location, or whether the population it is reaching is in some way unfairly biased.

Assessment looks to how the organisation is addressing issues of beneficiary awareness, access and inclusion, and any ways in which it can demonstrate success.

beneficiary awareness
Are beneficiaries aware of the organisation and the support it provides? Address may include: distribution of information about services (e.g. newsletters, website, hotline); media presence; leveraging community resources and networks for word of mouth.

beneficiary access
Can beneficiaries access the organisation's support? Access issues may include: transport (e.g. access by public transport); disabled access requirements; financial barriers; communication (where language is a problem); paperwork (forms that need to be filled in and could prove challenging).

beneficiary inclusion
Is the organisation's outreach inclusive, representative and diverse? This involves consideration of the make-up of the organisation's target population, and confirming the beneficiaries reached are a fair reflection of this (with regard to issues such as gender and ethnic minorities). Inclusion relates to awareness, access and uptake of support (i.e. are the people aware of and accessing services appropriately diverse?), and to successful outcomes (i.e. does the support result in successful outcomes for beneficiaries equally, or do certain groups do better or worse than others? If so, is there anything the organisation can do to make the success of its outcomes more inclusive?).

SCORING	
LOW	The organisation is not aware of whether or not it is reaching its target population of beneficiaries.
MEDIUM	The organisation has taken some steps to address issues of awareness, access and inclusion but obvious holes remain.
HIGH	The organisation promotes high levels of awareness and access among its beneficiaries and ensures the support it provides is inclusive.

2.1.2 Beneficiary Consultation

For an organisation's impact to be valid, it is crucial it engages with beneficiaries to ensure:

- the needs of beneficiaries are recognised
- the effects of activities upon beneficiaries are understood
- the resulting impact is something wanted and valued by beneficiaries themselves

Consultation offers the organisation a clear means to keep itself informed of the beneficiary perspective, and as such, the use of consultation is regarded as an important aspect of the validation of impact. Further to this, with direct experience of the issues under address, and as active service users, beneficiaries have a unique perspective upon the organisation's activities, and can offer valuable insights. Consultation is be a means to source beneficiary knowledge and views, and is most effective when approached as a dialogue.

Consultation may involve e.g. surveys, questionnaires, interviews, beneficiary discussion groups. A clear procedure for beneficiaries to feedback or make comments, suggestions or complaints to the organisation offers a further form of consultation. Offering beneficiaries a degree of choice as to how they interact with the organisation, and recording the choices made, offers a further, though somewhat weaker, form of consultation.

It is expected information from consultation feedsback into decision-making. The organisation may incorporate results from beneficiary consultation into its use of indicators, and in this way integrate it into the organisation's own monitoring and evaluation of impact.

The beneficiary perspective will be richer for understanding more about the organisation itself, as better informed beneficiaries are likely to be able to provide a more valuable response to consultation. This involves providing beneficiaries with information about the organisation's services, processes and results (including potentially copies of the organisation's reports and newsletters, which may be modified where appropriate to be accessible to beneficiaries).

Assessment looks to:

- the extent to which the organisation engages in beneficiary consultation
- the use to which information from consultation is then put (i.e. does it contribute to the organisation's understanding of what it is doing and influence direction?)
- the extent to which beneficiaries are themselves kept aware of the organisation's activities and results.

SCORING	
LOW	There is little or no evidence of beneficiary consultation.

MEDIUM	The organisation engages in beneficiary consultation, but consultation processes are not fully systematised and do not feed simply or directly into decision-making. Beneficiaries are given limited information.
HIGH	The organisation engages in systematic consultation processes and knows how to use the information it gathers. Beneficiaries are kept informed of the organisation's activities and invited to make suggestions.

2.1.3 Beneficiary Empowerment

A critical aspect of the organisation's impact is the extent to which it empowers beneficiaries to achieve their own personal goals. Beneficiary empowerment shifts the model from a provider-recipient relationship to one which engages beneficiaries to do more, and harnesses their energy and input in the generation of further impact.

Indications of Beneficiary Empowerment may include:

participation in activities
Participation looks to beneficiary participation in the organisation's activities, including, where appropriate, beneficiaries leading activities, and beneficiaries participating in creating, planning and developing activities. This may involve first ensuring beneficiaries have the knowledge and skills to participate, and supporting the development of these skills where necessary (e.g. awareness of issues, leadership skills, confidence).

use of capital
A significant aspect of beneficiary empowerment is the extent to which beneficiaries are empowered to direct the way in which capital invested in the organisation is used. This may take the form of beneficiary input in planning decisions regarding capital. Alternatively, there is a clear form of beneficiary empowerment over invested capital when that capital is used for on-lending to beneficiaries (e.g. microfinance, CDFIs), who then make decisions over how to use it.

defining impact
Through participation in defining impact, beneficiaries are empowered with respect to how the organisation understands what

it is achieving, and therefore how best to manage its activities. This may involve:
- beneficiary participation in the definition of progress
- beneficiary participation in identifying key measures and indicators used to observe impact
- beneficiary participation in the design and testing of surveys, questionnaires, or other methods used by the organisation to gather information on impact
- beneficiaries starting to measure their own progress

role with organisation
Organisations may empower beneficiaries to become fully involved in the organisation and its activities through providing beneficiaries with a distinct role. Integrating beneficiaries into the organisation's operations can help the organisation capture the skills and understanding of beneficiaries, and at the same time enable beneficiaries to use their experience of support productively.

Roles beneficiaries may take with the organisation include:
- volunteering
- employment within the organisation (including the question of whether beneficiaries are chiefly engaged in simpler operations, or if they are able to become involved in higher-level decision-making)
- engagement with advocacy (expressing the beneficiary perspective to external bodies)
- inclusion of beneficiaries on boards (or in appointing boards members)
- beneficiary ownership of the organisation (e.g. through shares, cooperatives structures)

Assessment of Beneficiary Empowerment considers the extent to which beneficiaries are being empowered by the organisation on the above four fronts.

SCORING	
LOW	Beneficiaries are not being demonstrably empowered on any of the above fronts.
MEDIUM	Beneficiaries are being empowered on one or two of the above fronts, though in a limited capacity.
HIGH	Beneficiaries are being substantially empowered (in so far as they are able) by the organisation on two or more of the above fronts.

2.1.4 Beneficiaries Connect

Through their outreach and services, social-purpose organisations are often able to connect with people who otherwise face exclusion — from networks, from services, and, not infrequently, from social contact. Connection can accordingly be a vital aspect of their work. But beyond the direct connection an organisation makes between itself and its beneficiaries, it may also play a role in supporting beneficiaries to connect with each other, share understanding and experiences, and build social networks of their own. The organisation may also support beneficiaries to build or rebuild social links with family, friends and support workers. This may take the form of facilitating communication among beneficiaries, setting up beneficiary groups, and helping organise beneficiary networks and interaction. The organisation may also help beneficiaries to share information by listening to and working with beneficiaries individually or in smaller groups, and then making this information more widely available within the beneficiary community (e.g. through forms of media such as a newsletter for beneficiaries, or a bulletin board). Supporting beneficiaries to develop their social universe can make a long-lasting contribution to impact, as beneficiaries build confidence and mutual support networks of their own.

SCORING	
LOW	The organisation does not contribute to building beneficiary social networks or the sharing of information among beneficiaries.
MEDIUM	The organisation's activities help beneficiaries to engage with each other and others, but the potential for these interactions to develop is under-realised, as is the potential for communicating information.
HIGH	The organisation actively fosters beneficiary social networks, and helps beneficiaries share information, knowledge and experiences with each other.

2.1.5 Beneficiary Satisfaction

The organisation may demonstrate that its services and impacts are valued by beneficiaries by showing evidence of beneficiary satisfaction.

SCORING	
LOW	There is no indication of beneficiary satisfaction, or only isolated quotations from individual beneficiaries.
MEDIUM	Beneficiary satisfaction is inferred through output indicators (e.g. retention rates, referrals from beneficiaries), but beyond quotations from individual beneficiaries, there is limited direct expression of satisfaction from beneficiaries themselves.
HIGH	Beneficiary satisfaction is clearly expressed by beneficiaries themselves in a structured fashion (e.g. from surveys) and supported by results from outputs indicators.

2.2 Beneficiary Impacts

Assessment of Beneficiary Impacts takes place across two fronts:

2.2.1 Matrix of Human, Social and Environmental Rights and Benefits
2.2.2 Unit Cost

2.2.1 Matrix of Human, Social and Environmental Rights and Benefits

The Matrix of Human, Social and Environmental Rights and Benefits is a tool for assessing the extent to which the organisation's activities penetrate the lives and environments of its beneficiaries, and drive the delivery of positive impact. An analysis of what the organisation is achieving is carried out against a matrix consisting of fifteen core social and environmental fields, whereby the degree to which benefits in each of the identified fields are realised provides an assessment of the depth of overall change achieved. Different organisations will, according to their own particular missions, find more or less resonance with the different fields — most likely achieving a strong address in one or two fields, with lighter impacts running across others.

The matrix comprises the following core fields:

a. Education and Family
b. Employment
c. Housing and Essential Needs
d. Economic Factors
e. Health
f. High Risk Behaviour
g. Care of Disabled and Older People
h. Safety and Community
i. Arts, Culture and Sports
j. Information, Understanding and Expression
k. Local Environment
l. Well-Being

m. Conservation and Biodiversity
n. Greenhouse Gas Emissions
o. Consumption, Waste, Pollution and Recycling

In assessing the overall impact of an organisation, it is important to consider not only the primary issue addressed, but also how that address is able to drive benefits in other areas. For example, an organisation focused on job creation most obviously relates to b. Employment, but through supporting its beneficiaries in finding work, it may drive significant further benefits in areas such as financial security (an aspect of d. Economic Factors) and confidence (an aspect of l. Well-Being). Similarly, an organisation dealing primarily with health issues (e. Health) may achieve positive outcomes for beneficiaries in areas such as access to employment (b. Employment), education (a. Education and Family), and managing at home (c. Housing and Essential Needs) by virtue of the improved health condition. Likewise, dealing with Pollution (o. Consumption, Waste, Pollution and Recycling) can drive benefits in terms of health, and so on.

This approach accords with a holistic concept of human development, whereby deep level changes made to a beneficiary's access to any one of a set of essential human values resonates outwards across the set. The ultimate interconnectedness of these values or fields is such that profound impacts upon beneficiaries' lives will be apparent on numerous fronts. Conversely, relatively shallow or light impacts on any one front are unlikely to lead to significant benefits on others. (For a more complete discussion of this idea, see the Overview in Part I, 3. MIAA: Development and Overview.)

Assessment looks to the organisation's total impact: i.e. not only its primary impacts, but also the subsequent or follow-on impacts that are generated as its outcomes permeate the lives of its beneficiaries and those around them. The extent to which these impacts can be acknowledged depends on the robustness with which they are linked to the organisation's immediate impacts, and the degree to which they are evidenced by the organisation through its measurement and reporting. Implied or inferred benefits score less highly than those which are fully demonstrated. (In relation to the organisation's subsequent impacts and links with primary impacts, see the discussion of scope of claimed outcomes in 1.3.1 Theory of Change.)

Assessment considers the organisation's impact against each field, with detailed analysis where appropriate (typically this will only be necessary for the primary fields in which an organisation is active). Assessment within the various fields is supported by and performed with reference to the indicator tables, located in 6. Appendix C: Beneficiary Perspective Indicator Tables.

a. Education and Family
Impacts advance beneficiary access to the right to education and the right to enjoy family life in a safe and supportive environment.
covers: education, parents, child and youth needs and basic care, marital and family support, women and domestic abuse

b. Employment
Impacts advance beneficiary access to the right to employment.
covers: employment, training and advice, support for professional advancement

c. Housing and Essential Needs
Impacts advance beneficiary access to the right to housing within a healthy and sustainable environment, and the right to adequate provisions regarding domestic and home needs.
covers: housing and essential needs

d. Economic Factors
Impacts advance beneficiary access to rights to economic means and security.
covers: access to financial services, financial security, financial management

e. Health
Impacts advance beneficiary access to the right to the highest attainable standard of physical and mental health.
covers: health services, health education and the promotion of healthy lifestyles

f. High Risk Behaviour
Impacts help beneficiaries manage high risk behaviour.
covers: offenders and ex-offenders, youth offending, substance abuse

g. Care of Disabled and Older People
Impacts advance the access of disabled and older people to the right to a healthy and fulfilling life and the right to be as independently capable as possible.
covers: disabled people, older people

h. Safety and Community
Impacts advance beneficiary access to the right to a sense of community, and the right to personal safety and freedom from discrimination.
covers: community, safety and crime

i. Arts, Culture and Sports
Impacts advance beneficiary access to the right to participation in cultural life including arts and sports.
covers: arts and culture, sports and recreation

j. Information, Understanding and Expression
Impacts advance beneficiary access to information and understanding regarding the issues under address, and access to the right to expression.
covers: communication within the sector, advocacy, beneficiary expression, public awareness

k. Local Environment
Impacts advance beneficiary access to the right to live in a healthy and sustainable local environment with adequate infrastructure and community space.
covers: quality of locality, local community buildings, local infrastructure, transport

l. Well-Being
Impacts advance the right to well-being.
covers: confidence, being able, being satisfied, feeling connected

m. Conservation and Biodiversity
Impacts advance the conservation of natural and cultural heritage, natural ecosystems, and biodiversity.
covers: sites of natural or historic value, biodiversity, research and education regarding conservation

n. Greenhouse Gas Emissions
Impacts serve to reduce global greenhouse gas emissions.
covers: sustainable agriculture, energy, green building, sustainable transport

o. Consumption, Waste, Pollution and Recycling
Impacts safeguard natural resources and promote environmentally responsible practices
covers: consumption, waste and recycling, pollution and clean up, water

A score is awarded against each field within the matrix. Organisations may pick up points in any field up to a weighted maximum (see 4. Appendix A: Weighted Impact Scoresheet).

SCORING	
LOW	Beneficiaries experience no positive change with regard to these rights or this field of impact.
MEDIUM	Beneficiaries experience some positive change, though this is likely to be a secondary or knock-on impact (as opposed to a primary impact delivered directly by the organisation). The strength of data collection around the impact may be weak and the change itself partially inferred rather than fully evidenced. There may also be other contributing factors.
HIGH	Beneficiaries experience major positive change with regard to these rights or this field. The change is clearly evidenced, and strongly linked to the organisation's activities, which are the primary drivers of the change.

2.2.2 Unit Cost

The Unit Cost assessment looks to the scale at which the impacts identified through the matrix are being rolled out. While the assessment in 2.2.1 Matrix of Human, Social and Environmental Rights and Benefits asks essentially what is — and what is the depth of — the change; 2.2.2 Unit Cost asks: what is the breadth of that change?

The breadth of change is reviewed in relation to the size of the social-purpose organisation, taken in this case to mean its financial size. The organisation's capital intensity is most obviously indicated by looking at the impact in relation to the turnover or gross operating expenditure required to carry out the impact-generating activities. However there may be considerable fixed assets involved (e.g. properties) that relate to the volume of capital being drawn on to achieve the impact, and which are likely to have implications for the scalability of the impact in relation to new injections of capital. The size is therefore taken to be whichever is larger of the organisation's turnover and total balance sheet. For organisations looking to raise significant volumes of new capital (e.g. through an investment offering), the size of the capital raise should be factored into calculations regarding the prospective new impacts.

Using this financial size, the Unit Cost consideration is a then form of ratio: that of the total impact delivered to the total capital drawn upon.

Calculations on the social benefits side can be addressed using the idea of the number of "lives touched". A "lives touched" estimate of the unit cost looks at how many beneficiaries the organisation is reaching, and divides the financial size by this number to arrive at a figure for "dollars per life touched". Organisations dealing primarily with reductions in greenhouse gas emissions should likewise be able to produce a unit cost figure for dollars per tonne of CO_2 not emitted. For organisations whose chief impacts relate neither to the lives of beneficiaries nor to tonnes of CO_2 (or equivalents) offset (e.g. biodiversity programmes), a unit cost may be calculated for the most relevant output.

Given the different units involved, these figures are not suitable for direct numeric transformation into scores. Variance among counting mechanisms may also be a factor. In particular, the way in which social impact organisations count the number of lives touched can vary considerably, and it is therefore necessary for the analyst to scrutinise the quality of the numbers produced by the organisation, as well as calculating the ratio. For example, an organisation may decide to include the immediate family members of its direct beneficiaries in its calculation of lives touched, on the grounds that family members are also benefitting from the impacts achieved. This may allow an organisation to quintuple its figure for lives touched, but in so doing, the organisation is not automatically achieving five times as much breadth of change as another organisation which does not perform this particular piece of accounting arithmetic.

Ratios of unit cost must be reviewed critically and compared to prevailing ratios across the social-purpose universe, and against relevant class or sector ratios. It is also necessary in doing this to consider the organisation's own accounting methods in calculating its unit cost (or number of lives touched). For organisations which do not offer a figure, the analyst may make an informed assessment.

The most appropriate measure for unit cost calculations can be arrived at by referring back to the matrix analysis of 2.2.1, and asking how widely the specific changes identified and scored positively in the matrix are being achieved. For example, if an organisation is focused on e. Health, the most appropriate unit cost calculation would focus on how many people are receiving the relevant health benefits. If an organisation's impact is apparent on multiple fronts (e.g. through programmes relating to c. Housing and Essential Needs and b. Employment), it may be necessary to consider the unit cost being achieved on these different fronts, and calculate an average proportionally (i.e. proportional to the volume of capital being directed to each).

Unit cost is a field where usable benchmarks are yet to be fully established. However by performing a unit cost calculation for each assessment made (and including details of how it has been arrived at), it is possible to build up a database of the kinds of unit costs achieved by organisations operating in different sectors and geographies, and to progress toward a more developed sense of comparative efficiency.

It is worth noting that in this calculation, almost inevitably organisations operating in the developing world achieve significantly higher ratios than those operating in fully industrialised countries. This is because the beneficiaries involved are generally that much poorer, and the purchasing power of invested dollars in those economies that much greater. Consequently developing world operations are likely to be able to score higher on this consideration. While in some ways this represents a bias within one part of the assessment system, it is legitimised by the one fundamental unit social accounting has to refer to — that of a single human life. In this sense, more breadth is indeed available for each dollar invested in the developing world. Furthermore it should be remembered that this is one consideration within the overall analysis, and that organisations with excellent — even if capital intensive — operations in non-developing world countries are still able to achieve high overall scores (while receiving medium to low scores on this particular consideration).

Assessment looks to the unit cost of the organisation's impact, and scores it in relation to:

- accuracy and transparency
- efficiency within the sector
- overall breadth achieved

SCORING	
LOW	The organisation provides little or incomplete information relating to its own breadth of change, and no opportunity to relate it to others. Assessment by the analyst for an organisation focused on social benefits suggests a unit cost of more than US$10,000 per life touched.
MEDIUM	The organisation engages with thinking about its breadth of change and presents relevant information, which suggests that it is maintaining prevailing sector ratios. The estimated unit cost for an organisation focused on social benefits is between US$1,000 and US$10,000 per life touched.
HIGH	The organisation effectively demonstrates its breadth of change, and the efficiency of its breadth in comparison with the sector in which it is active. The unit cost for an organisation focused on social benefits is shown to be below US$1,000 per life touched.

3. WIDER IMPACT

Wider Impact looks at how the organisation's impact plays out in the world beyond the organisation and its immediate beneficiaries. The essential question is: *How do your impacts relate to the greater world around them?*

The assessment is divided into five sections:

    3.1 Additionality
    3.2 Impact Multipliers
    3.3 Game Change
    3.4 Impact Risk
    3.5 Responsible Management

The Wider Impact summary table (see overleaf) lays out the considerations that comprise the assessment. These are then worked through one by one over the succeeding pages, which detail how to understand and score each point. The full MIAA Impact Scoresheet is given in 4. Appendix A: Weighted Impact Scoresheet.

INVESTING FOR GOOD

3	**WIDER IMPACT**	
3.1	**Additionality**	
3.1.1	Impact over the BAU	
	How do the organisation's impacts compare with the BAU scenario? *CHECK FOR: other service providers, government, the commercial sector, beneficiary progress without intervention*	
3.1.2	Cost Benefits	
	Does the organisation's impact lead to significant cost benefits through direct savings, avoided costs or increased revenues? *CHECK FOR: savings in direct expenditure, avoidance of potential costs, increased revenues*	
3.2	**Impact Multipliers**	
3.2.1	Economic Boost	
	a. Direct Spending Does the organisation's direct spending boost the local economy?	
	b. Recirculation and New Spending Do the organisation's activities generate significant onspending and new spending in the local economy?	
	c. Direct Investment Do the investment structures and activities of the organisation leverage further direct investment into its projects?	
	d. Local Value Does the organisation's work attract further capital into the wider community or sector, thus contributing to a general boost in local value?	
3.2.2	Knowledge Boost	
	a. Sharing Information Within the Sector Does the organisation actively share information and collaborate with other sector organisations?	
	b. Representing the Sector to Government and Business Does the organisation engage with government and business over the issues it seeks to address?	
	c. Raising Public Awareness Does the organisation work to raise public awareness and understanding?	
3.3	**Game Change**	
3.3.1	Innovation of Approach	
	Is the organisation developing new innovations with potentially game changing outcomes?	
3.3.2	Pioneering of New Models	
	Is the organisation pioneering new models to inspire widespread change?	
3.4	**Impact Risk**	
3.4.1	Diversification of Impacts	
	Are the organisation's activities and impacts appropriately diversified?	

3.4.2	Policy Dependency	
	Is the organisation dependent on particular policies which are at risk of change?	
3.5	**Responsible Management**	
3.5.1	Responsible Management	
	Do the organisation's operations accord with the principles of responsible management? *CHECK FOR: employment, open and democratic processes, volunteer policy, environmental policy*	

3.1 Additionality

Additionality addresses the question: to what extent are the benefits an organisation is achieving adding something truly new — i.e. something that wouldn't have happened otherwise?

Implicit in the concept of impact is the existence of a situation that the impact is hitting, and thereby effecting a change. But the original situation may itself not be static. If the situation is developing in some way on its own, then even without the impact, there would still have been some change. Therefore to understand the real change created by an impact, it is necessary to look at the difference between the situation with the impact, and the situation as it would have been had the impact not occurred. The change created is said to be additional in so far as it exceeds any change that would have happened anyway.

The question of additionality addresses this alternative scenario of "what would have happened anyway" — sometimes also referred to as the "deadweight scenario", the "counterfactual case", or, as is used henceforth, the business-as-usual or BAU scenario. As social and environmental impacts take place in a profoundly dynamic world, the BAU scenario can present significant changes of its own. However it presents also a challenge, as it is necessarily hypothetical. There is no perfect "control experiment" for how things would have looked without the organisation's intervention, and consideration of additionality therefore requires some research into what this alternative BAU scenario might look like.

For social-purpose organisations, an address of the question of additionality — i.e. of what would have happened to their beneficiaries had their activities not taken place, or their services not been available — is an important aspect of gaining a true picture of their overall impact. Organisations which consider additionality in their impact reporting are therefore regarded as more transparent and more complete in this regard. The BAU scenario as presented by the organisation should show some evidence of research, and, where possible, be substantiated by real information (e.g. what happens in similar situations where the organisation is not present). In the absence of any address of additionality on the part of the organisation, the analyst is forced to construct a BAU scenario from available information (e.g. from other organisations working in the sector and from the initial conditions), and compare it with the organisation's reported impact.

Assessment of Additionality takes place on two fronts:

3.1.1 Impact over the BAU
3.1.2 Cost Benefits

3.1.1 Impact Over the BAU

Assessment of Impact Over the BAU looks to the extent to which the organisation's impacts outperform what would have been achieved under BAU conditions. Understanding the BAU scenario requires consideration of forces outside of the organisation in the area in which it operates, and comparison with what happens in other potentially similar areas in which it does not operate.

Assessment focuses on four aspects of the BAU:

other service providers
The BAU takes account of other service providers, and their potential outreach to the organisation's beneficiaries. First to consider is whether the beneficiaries reached by the organisation have (or had) access to other service providers, and if so, how do their services and outcomes compare? Also pertinent is the question of whether, had the organisation not been active in this area, another service provider would have stepped in. (This may be the case where there is a specific government contract for service provision that is bid for competitively, or in sectors or areas where there is a crowding of impact organisations.) The additionality of the organisation's impact is the impact over and above what would have been achieved by other (competing) service providers.

government
The BAU incorporates the default government response to the problem that the organisation is tackling. Assessment turns to what government services beneficiaries would most likely have accessed had the organisation not been active, and compares these with the outcomes achieved by the organisation.

the commercial sector
The BAU may also be influenced by the activities of the commercial sector. The question posed is: how, in the absence of the organisation,

the mainstream commercial sector responds to the organisation's beneficiaries? For beneficiaries who are completely excluded from the mainstream there would be no response, but for others there may be (possibly less favourable) commercial alternatives or outcomes.

beneficiary progress without intervention
In the absence of intervention from the organisation or other significant actors, there may be evidence to suggest beneficiaries are nevertheless able to make progress on their own. For example, an employment-focused organisation may provide a programme to help unemployed people find work, but it is possible that without the programme, a number of these people would have found jobs anyway. This aspect of the BAU forms a baseline of beneficiary progress without intervention.

Assessment looks to the additionality of the organisation's impact over the BAU (as observed in relation to these four aspects), with organisations showing substantial additionality being regarded as higher impact.

SCORING	
LOW	The organisation does not consider the BAU in its reporting. Assessment by the analyst suggests reasons to believe the BAU compromises the additionality of the organisation's impact.
MEDIUM	The organisation gives some consideration to the BAU in its reporting, and is able to demonstrate that while there may be some compromise, the impact is still additional OR the organisation gives little consideration to the BAU, but its impacts are clearly additional.
HIGH	The organisation demonstrates convincingly that its impacts are significantly additional to the BAU.

3.1.2 Cost Benefits

Consideration of Cost Benefits looks specifically to the economic costs of the BAU scenario. These are costs that lie not with beneficiaries, but most often with government and society at large (economic benefits relating directly to beneficiaries are treated in 2.2.1-d Economic Benefits within the Beneficiary Perspective analysis). An organisation's impact, in addition to generating specific human or environmental benefits, may well also deliver significant wider cost benefits by dealing with an expensive problem.

Assessment focuses on three aspects:

savings in direct expenditure
Savings in direct expenditure are most commonly achieved when an organisation's impact serves to bring people who were dependent on government benefits either off benefits, or to a lowered level of dependency. Examples include: an employment-focused organisation that puts people who were drawing unemployment benefits into work; or a health or disability-focused organisation that enhances the capacity of people to manage without benefits.

Where savings in direct expenditure take place it is often relatively simple for an organisation to calculate the savings, and present them as an economic return to society. (N.B. It is important to adjust the savings for the BAU — i.e. to deduct those savings for the proportion of people that would most likely have otherwise made their way off benefits.)

avoidance of potential costs
Avoidance of potential costs refers to expensive negative potential outcomes that are neutralised through the organisation's impact. Examples include: an organisation working with ex-offenders who, without the organisation's impact, would be more likely to reoffend and thus incur significant government costs; or an organisation working with at risk youth who, without the organisation's impact, would be more likely to drop out of school, fail to find employment, and enter into a downward economic spiral.

Calculating avoided potential costs is likely to be a more speculative process than calculating savings in direct expenditure as it relies on estimating the cost implications of events that have not taken place. The organisation may nevertheless be able to produce a reasonable figure for avoided costs based on the cost of similar events taking place elsewhere, and the prevailing rates of negative outcomes under BAU conditions.

increased revenues
In addition to making savings and/or avoiding costs, an organisation's impact may generate increased government revenues through improving productivity among beneficiaries, leading to increased economic activity and thereby increased tax revenues. These are likely

to be small in comparison with the savings in direct expenditure or the avoided costs, but may nevertheless be counted by the organisation in its calculation of cost benefits.

The calculation of cost benefits is inevitably somewhat conjectural, and it is therefore important to scrutinise the organisation's analysis to ensure that it is reasonable and well-evidenced. Cost benefits may be very considerable, especially where the impacts imply long term sustainable change among beneficiaries who otherwise present significant expenses to society. However these need to be considered against how concrete the cost benefits really are. Assessment looks to both the size of the cost benefits and to how robustly they can be accounted for.

SCORING	
LOW	The organisation's impact presents no particular cost benefits (or only increased tax revenues without any significant savings or avoided costs to government or society).
MEDIUM	The organisation's impact presents cost benefits through either savings in direct expenditure or avoided costs. However these may be weakly accounted for, indirect (e.g. taking place at several removes from the organisation's direct operating activities), or not significantly additional to the BAU.
HIGH	The organisation clearly demonstrates significant cost benefits to government and society as a result of its impact.

3.2 Impact Multipliers

Consideration of Impact Multipliers looks to how the organisation's impact plays out into society at large, and specifically, the extent to which it generates further positive benefits as it goes. Certain kinds of impact may create chains of self-multiplying impacts and benefits, either through being recirculated within a community, or through being passed on via networks to a widening body of people.

Impact multiplication presents itself in two key ways: as an economic boost, whereby economic aspects of the organisation's activities recirculate and multiply; and as a knowledge boost, whereby the organisation stimulates wider understanding through the provision of information. These create the two fronts for assessments:

> 3.2.1 Economic Boost
> 3.2.2 Knowledge Boost

3.2.1 Economic Boost

Alongside their primary impacts, all organisations, through their operations, have an economic impact in the areas in which they are active. The Economic Boost measure looks to the ways in which these impacts develop and multiply, driving further benefits for local or beneficiary communities.

Consideration of the organisation's economic boost looks to the quantitative values that the organisation can produce to demonstrate the economic boost it is delivering. However these values exhibit qualitative differences — in terms of how precisely they can be calculated, and how definitively they can be attributed to the organisation's activities. Assessment views the contribution the organisation is making to any discernible economic boost, and considers both how well supported the contribution is (in terms of evidence linking it to the organisation's activities), and how significant it is (i.e. the total value of the economic boost).

Assessment takes place across four fronts:

> a. Direct Spending
> b. Recirculation and New Spending

c. Direct Investment
d. Local Value

A. DIRECT SPENDING

The organisation may provide an economic boost through focusing its spending in the local area and among the beneficiary community. This can manifest through targeted use of local suppliers and service providers. The organisation may also hire locally, boosting employment for local people. In addition to hiring, the organisation may offer training and volunteering opportunities for local people, enhancing local skills and thereby, local productivity.

Direct Spending of this kind can be calculated in terms of the financial value of local contracts and spending, and the number and value of local jobs and volunteering or training opportunities created.

SCORING	
LOW	The organisation does not make any particular effort to direct its spending or hiring within the local or beneficiary community.
MEDIUM	The organisation is aware of the principle of spending and hiring within the local or beneficiary community, but is vague about moving on it, or how much it really does.
HIGH	The organisation has a clear strategy to encourage spending and hiring within the local or beneficiary community. It regards this as a part of its impact, and tracks it accordingly.

B. RECIRCULATION AND NEW SPENDING

Recirculation considers the ways in which economic activity generated by the organisation continues to recirculate among beneficiaries and the local community beyond its initial disbursement, providing expanding opportunities for an increasing number of people. Recirculation may occur through onspending by beneficiaries who have been economically advanced by the organisation's activities (e.g. found employment, gained access to credit, hired new staff themselves). Equally there may be local onspending by the people and local businesses who benefit from the organisation's direct spending (see above).

The organisation may also bring new spending into the community through attracting visitors (e.g. relatives of people in care, tourists visiting a conservation area). Visitor spending creates a further line of potential economic multiplication within the local economy.

Increased productivity and new spending may also be freed up by the organisation through the provision of respite care. Organisations which offer respite to family members and carers may provide those people with the opportunity to take more control of their lives, and thereby boost their local economic activity.

Calculation of Recirculation and New Spending is more difficult than that of Direct Spending. Economic analysis can however provide a picture of how significant the economic contribution of recirculation and new spending generated by the organisation's activities is. Short of full economic analysis, consideration can still be given to the influence of the organisation in this regard.

SCORING	
LOW	The organisation's impact does not influence recirculation or new spending within the local or beneficiary community.
MEDIUM	The organisation's impact does play a role in boosting the local or beneficiary community economy through recirculated or new spending. The impact however is light, and is not something the organisation has particularly considered.
HIGH	The organisation's impact gives a significant boost to the local or beneficiary economy through recirculated or new spending. The organisation regards this as part of its impact, and accordingly gives some account of how significant the contribution is.

C. DIRECT INVESTMENT

Direct Investment looks to the extent to which the organisation provides an economic boost through leveraging further investment into its activities.

One way this may be achieved is through the structuring of an investment product. For example, an investment with a subordinated layer of debt may be used to leverage further investment from more mainstream investors, who are prepared to enter into the upper layers of the structure. In this way the subordinated layer acts to multiply the investment capital reaching beneficiaries.

Another form of direct investment multiplication may come through the organisation engaging in co-investing. This is most relevant to funds or lending organisations, who may use their own investment capital to attract other investors to invest in their target businesses (e.g. SMEs in economically deprived areas, green businesses), and thus multiply the total invested capital. The fund or lending organisation may alternatively provide impact capital to help establish small businesses and ventures which, as they grow to scale, are then able to attract mainstream capital (a form of deferred investment multiplication).

The multiplication of direct investment in a structured investment offering can be calculated directly. Funds and lending organisations that achieve investment multiplication through co-investing can likewise look at their co-investments to calculate the level of investment multiplication. Deferred investment multiplication through investments into businesses seeded by the organisation is best demonstrated via a track record.

As well as the volume of additional direct investment, it is necessary to consider the extent to which this is leveraged specifically by the organisation. The organisation may use particular structures to attract mainstream investors who otherwise would not be investing in the sector. Alternatively the additional investment may come from likewise socially-motivated investors, who are more pairing with the organisation than being specifically leveraged by them (i.e. they would be investing in the sector anyway). Multiplication of the former kind is assessed to be providing a greater economic boost.

SCORING	
LOW	The organisation does not leverage further direct investment.
MEDIUM	The organisation engages structures and practices that bring further direct investment to its beneficiaries. However the additional investment is either small, or is coming from other socially-motivated investors (i.e. investors who would be investing in the sector anyway).
HIGH	The organisation is clearly leveraging substantial additional direct investment. The leveraged investment capital is coming from investors who would otherwise not be investing in the sector or among this group of beneficiaries.

D. LOCAL VALUE

Through its work an organisation may provide a wider economic boost by enhancing local value. The organisation's activities may kick start or contribute to local regeneration efforts, as well as drawing attention to the area or sector, and thereby building confidence, and encouraging others to invest locally or start businesses also aimed at serving the organisation's target beneficiaries.

Enhanced local value may be observed through: an increase in investment in the local area, beneficiary community, or sector by new businesses or social enterprises opening up; new government initiatives being introduced; and new investments in local infrastructure. In each of these cases, assessment looks for evidence that the businesses or government actors involved identify the organisation's work as a contributing factor in the decision to invest. The total value of the investment or number of new business or social enterprises can be calculated with this in mind.

A rise in local value may also be witnessed through an increase in property or land values, though to be connected to the organisation's work these have to be shown to be over and above the BAU, and clearly tied to the more tangible aspects of the organisation's contributions to local value.

SCORING	
LOW	The organisation's impact does not influence local value.
MEDIUM	The local value where the organisation's activities take place is clearly rising, and it is likely the organisation's presence is a part of this. However either the rise is not very significant, or the organisation is more following the rise than leading it (e.g. has come into the area as part of a larger regeneration plan).
HIGH	The organisation's impact is clearly contributing to an increase in local value, with significant numbers of new businesses or government initiatives coming into the area or sector, in part as a result of the organisation's work.

3.2.2 Knowledge Boost

Assessment of Knowledge Boost considers the way in which the organisation contributes to a wider awareness and understanding of the problem it seeks to address. Indeed a lack of knowledge about the problem may be an important part of the problem itself, and the organisation's knowledge boost can therefore be a significant aspect of its wider impact.

Through on-the-ground work with beneficiary communities, social-purpose organisations are in a unique position to gather information and develop an understanding — in terms of both community needs and community potential. Disseminating this knowledge can be an excellent way to raise awareness, inspire multilateral activity, and inform the practices of other organisations. Effective communication with business and governmental bodies, as well as with local environments and the wider public, can play a pivotal role.

As with economic factors, the knowledge disseminated by an organisation can both recirculate and multiply, driving wider impacts across large populations.

Assessment of Knowledge Boost takes place on three fronts:

a. Sharing Information Within the Sector
b. Representing the Sector to Government and Business
c. Raising Public Awareness

For organisations whose primary impacts (as opposed to wider impacts) are knowledge-focused — for example advocacy or campaign groups, or organisations focused on providing informational support to sector organisations — there is a detailed treatment of knowledge-related impacts in 2. Beneficiary Perspective (see 2.2.1-j Information, Understanding and Expression and the related indicator tables in 6. Appendix C: Beneficiary Perspective Indicator Tables). This applies where the key beneficiary perspective relates to the information provided by the organisation. The assessment of Knowledge Boost here in 3. Wider Impacts considers the organisation's knowledge impacts from the perspective of those beyond the organisation and its immediate beneficiaries, and the utilisation of knowledge derived from primary operations to multiply and boost understanding elsewhere.

The organisation is assessed for its level of engagement with knowledge boosting activities, and the extent of its demonstrable impact in this regard.

A. SHARING INFORMATION WITHIN THE SECTOR

Sharing information within the sector implies three key audiences: other sector organisations, capital providers and beneficiaries. Communication with providers and beneficiaries is covered chiefly by the organisation's reporting (see 1.3.3 Impact Reporting) and beneficiary engagement processes (see 2.1.2 Beneficiary Consultation). Information shared with other sector organisations, covered here, may relate to:

- the organisation's research on beneficiary needs and issues
- the organisation's approach, activities and techniques
- the organisation's results and key successes

The organisation may share information through publications and information on its website. A more proactive approach to boosting sectoral knowledge may include engagement with sector bodies and network activities, as well as attendance at conferences and events. Collaborations and partnerships with other sector organisations can be seen as further evidence of the organisation engaging with the sector to drive understanding.

The key aims of sharing information within the sector are to increase understanding, spread innovations and new ideas, and to develop theories of best practice.

SCORING	
LOW	The organisation has limited contact with other organisations and does not distribute information about its own research or activities.
MEDIUM	The organisation publishes information about its own activities on its website and engages with sector networks. This is however a low priority.
HIGH	The organisation publishes information about its research and activities on its website and elsewhere, is actively participating in networks, and prides itself on being a thought leader in the sector.

B. REPRESENTING THE SECTOR TO GOVERNMENT AND BUSINESS

The organisation may also play a role in representing the sector and the interests of its beneficiaries to government and business. This may occur on the local level through involvement with community groups and in local planning issues. On a larger scale the organisation may be involved in helping form government policy through: lobbying and making recommendations; submitting research; holding appointed positions within advisory groups; and contributing to government policy documents.

Likewise the organisation may have a knowledge-boosting effect in communicating with business — raising issues where relevant, and potentially forming strategic partnerships or sponsorships.

The organisation's activities on this front may be observed through:

- changes in government or company policy
- contributions from or references to the organisation in relevant policy documents
- roles taken in partnership with government or business, or roles in relevant advisory or planning bodies
- increased funding or non-financial support from government or business for the sector as a result of the organisation pressing for it

Organisations active in developing world countries may play a wider role in boosting knowledge through offering advice to government and business as to how to structure sector development — for example in helping with the legal frameworks or international standards.

SCORING	
LOW	The organisation does not play a role in representing the sector or its beneficiaries to government or business.
MEDIUM	The organisation takes part in local planning.
HIGH	The organisation communicates with government around policy and coordinates its efforts with business, resulting in tangible recommendations, agreements or changes at regional, national or international levels.

C. RAISING PUBLIC AWARENESS

The organisation may play a further role in raising public awareness of the needs and issues it deals with. This may be observed through the organisation's publicity and media presence (e.g. number of pieces published in the media relating to the organisation's work), as well as its presence at public events and success in garnering high-profile support.

Efforts to raise public awareness may result in increased donations and inquiries to the organisation (e.g. through calls, website hits etc.). In addition the organisation may monitor levels of public awareness and public attitudes toward the problem it seeks to address.

SCORING	
LOW	The organisation makes no significant contribution to an increase in public awareness.
MEDIUM	The organisation looks to raise public awareness locally.
HIGH	The organisation engages with the public on a large scale, has a significant public voice (e.g. in the media), and contributes to shaping public understanding around the issues addressed.

3.3 Game Change

Social-purpose organisations often pursue new and highly innovative approaches to social and environmental problems, and one of the forms of social return potentially available to capital providers is that of having supported the growth of a pioneer idea or model. An organisation is described as pioneering if it is forging a new path that others may later follow — thereby offering the potential to bring about a game change in thinking and behaviour, both within the sector and possibly beyond.

Assessment of Game Change takes place on two fronts:

3.3.1 Innovation of Approach
3.3.2 Pioneering of New Models

3.3.1 Innovation of Approach

Assessment of the innovation of approach looks to the organisation's core business for innovation. This may include scientific research (e.g. papers published), new technologies, and new ideas or strategies for addressing a problem. Organisations are considered for their activity in developing new innovations, and for the potential for these innovations to present replicable new approaches that could be rolled out more widely, ultimately yielding game changing outcomes.

SCORING	
LOW	The organisation is using an established approach.
MEDIUM	The organisation is developing new ideas, approaches, or technologies. However these either present relatively small departures from the existing models, or have limited potential to inspire wider change.
HIGH	The organisation is developing new ideas, approaches or technologies with truly game changing potential.

3.3.2 Pioneering of New Models

Assessment of the pioneering of new models looks to the organisation's role in pursuing activities in a pioneering fashion. The core business ideas or technologies may or may not have been developed by the organisation itself, but the key to pioneering on this front is the application. The organisation may take an existing business model and pioneer it in a new geographic region (in turn inspiring other organisations to follow, and thus creating a game change through opening a new market). Alternatively it may have formulated a new model itself, and be working to pioneer it elsewhere through setting up franchises or actively encouraging its adoption (e.g. through promoting the model, visiting possible areas of application, offering advice to people interested in using the model).

Assessment considers the organisation's engagement with pioneering activities, and the potential of these to leverage further investments, follower organisations, and widespread change (i.e. beyond the organisation's direct field of operations).

SCORING	
LOW	The organisation is active within well-defined boundaries with no particular pioneering aspects.
MEDIUM	The organisation is applying new ideas in new areas alongside a relatively small group of others ("early adopters"), and as such is playing a part in helping establish their viability.
HIGH	The organisation is pioneering the application of a significantly new idea or model, or is breaking ground with an idea in a new geographic area, with significant potential for others to follow.

3.4 Impact Risk

In addition to considering the impacts themselves, it is important to consider the level of associated impact risk. Impact risk differs from financial risk in that rather than looking at risk from the perspective of protecting financial value, it takes the perspective of protecting social value and the ongoing achievement of impact.

There is considerable overlap between impact risk and financial risk in so far as anything that would result in the financial collapse of the organisation would equally terminate its ability to achieve impact. This aspect of risk is addressed in the Confidence consideration (see Part I, 3. MIAA: Development and Overview). Equally impact may be at risk if it conflicts with the financial viability of the organisation, and is addressed in 1.3.4 Balance and Alignment. The Wider Impacts address of impact risk looks to the risk posed by factors emanating from outside the organisation (i.e. other than the organisation either failing financially or reneging on the primacy of its mission).

Assessment takes place on two fronts:

3.4.1 Diversification of Impacts
3.4.2 Policy Dependency

3.4.1 Diversification of Impacts

Organisations whose operations are focused on a narrow range of impacts are considered less well diversified. For on-lending organisations, a diversified portfolio of investments and a strong deal-flow of new investable options is an important part of impact risk mitigation. Venture capital funds planning to make a smaller number of investments in early stage organisations are likely to face a comparatively greater risk of loss of impact due to a proposed investment falling through.

Organisations which are themselves the primary generators of impact may equally be more or less well diversified. Diversification may take the form of multiple centres with geographical diversity. There may also be a diversity of approaches through which impacts are achieved. Inflexible commitments to a small number of fixed assets, technologies or products may expose the impact to higher levels of risk.

Assessment looks to the organisation's diversification of impacts, the stability of the markets and environments in which it operates, and any steps it has taken to identify and mitigate risks on these fronts.

SCORING	
LOW	The organisation's impacts are not diversified.
MEDIUM	The organisation's impacts show limited diversity, either in terms of what they do or geographically (though most likely not both).
HIGH	The organisation's impacts are well diversified, both in terms of what they do and geographically.

3.4.2 Policy Dependency

The ability of the organisation to achieve impact may be dependent on a specific sympathetic policy environment. This may relate to favourable government regulations within a particular marketplace (e.g. subsidies and targets), or direct government contracts for the supply of services (e.g. with local authorities).

Assessment looks to the organisation's exposure to risk from government policy change, the stability of the government concerned and the specific policies involved, and any steps the organisation has taken to identify and mitigate risks on this front.

SCORING	
LOW	The organisation is exposed to policy risk and has taken little or no steps to mitigate the risk.
MEDIUM	The organisation has some exposure to policy risk, but this is mitigated either through steps the organisation has taken (e.g. diversification, inherent flexibility), or through the essential stability of the policies themselves.
HIGH	The organisation has no exposure to policy risk.

3.5 Responsible Management

Assessment of Responsible Management looks to the organisation's internal policies and procedures to verify these are carried out in a socially and environmentally responsible manner. These are secondary considerations to the organisation's primary purpose and impact — that of pursuing activities which deliver impact-generating outputs and outcomes to beneficiaries. However within the context in which the organisation operates, it equally has an impact on its staff and on the environment, and this is accordingly considered as part of the Wider Impact.

Assessment of the organisation on this front is largely derived from standard notions of corporate social responsibility, and focuses on four aspects:

employment
Consideration of employment covers:
- terms of employment (including appropriate provision for benefits, leave etc.)
- employee wages (considered in relation to comparable local wages and wage equity within the organisation — i.e. the ratio of the lowest to the highest wage)
- employee safety
- employee training (whereby employees are able to develop their knowledge and skills)
- fair and non-discriminatory hiring policy

open and democratic processes
Open and democratic processes ensure employees have a voice within the organisation, and opportunities to express themselves through formal feedback and complaints procedures and, where appropriate, opportunities for collective bargaining.

volunteer policy
(For organisations that use volunteers.) The organisation's volunteer policy ensures someone is responsible for managing volunteers, and that volunteer feedback and review processes are in place.

INVESTING FOR GOOD

environmental policy

The organisation shows a responsible approach to the environment, covering:
- the existence of an environmental policy
- the monitoring of environmental performance
- communication of environmental goals and achievements within the organisation and externally
- compliance with basic measures (energy saving through switching off appliances, recycling, the use where possible of greener transport options, the use where possible of green buildings)

SCORING	
LOW	The organisation does not demonstrate responsible management.
MEDIUM	The organisation demonstrates responsible management on some but not all points.
HIGH	The organisation demonstrates best practice with respect to socially and environmentally responsible management.

4. APPENDIX A: WEIGHTED IMPACT SCORESHEET

The Weighted Impact Scoresheet (see below) lays out the maximum potential score available on each consideration, and the section by section totals. The scores awarded relate to the LOW, MEDIUM and HIGH guidelines set out in the methodology, while leaving some room for nuance on the part of the analyst. The smallest scoring increment is a half point, and so, for example, on a consideration weighted with 3 points, an assessment of LOW could translate to a score of 0, 0.5, or 1; MEDIUM to 1.5 or 2; and HIGH to 2.5 or 3 — according to the analyst's direct understanding of the organisation they are looking at, and the shades of impact performance that it presents. The LOW / MEDIUM / HIGH guidelines in effect provide stable markers in relation to which a reasoned assessment is made. Thus scoring works in accordance with the principles set out in Part I for an impact methodology that is at once consistent and sensitive to case-by-case analysis.

The weightings set the relative importance of each consideration to the overall assessment — most obviously in the sense that considerations loaded with more points have greater sway over the total, and thereby over the rating produced. However, while this gives the weightings considerable apparent influence, it is still the larger structure of the methodology that determines how the analysis is carried out, and embedded within this structure are a number of powerful factors regarding weighting. Firstly, the multiperspective approach, and the corroboration effect it sets up (see discussion in Part I, 3. MIAA: Development and Overview), allows impacts to pick up points in multiple sections. This considerably limits the relevance of the weight of any one consideration, as rather, it is the quality of multidimensionality that is awarded an implicit weight of its own. Further to this, the composition of the analysis within the specific sections defines where and how the organisation is able to score. Areas which are given an in depth analytical treatment, with numerous scoring considerations (and therefore numerous opportunities to score), naturally amass weight; areas where the analysis is less detailed and there are fewer considerations to address, tend to be lighter.

Given this degree of in-built weighting, the actual mechanics of setting the number of points available on each consideration is more toward the fine tuning end of the methodology. And indeed, the weightings presented here have been tuned through practical application and experience. This has been a matter of assigning weights, scoring organisations, reviewing scores, and reweighting where necessary. The reference point when balancing the weightings is provided by the analysis itself.

It is crucial that the results produced by an analytical methodology remain congruent with the reality revealed by the analytical process (this relationship breaks down when the analysis and the result seem to be pointing in opposite directions — e.g. analysis shows an organisation to be high impact, yet the weighted score awards it a rating of 3; or analysis shows an organisation to be low impact, yet the weighted score awards it a rating of 1). This reality-revealed-through-analysis is captured as the analyst, in working through the methodology, assigns not only a score on each consideration, but also makes a note — a kind of "answer" to the "question" that each consideration poses. Gathering together these notes or answers forms the basis for a critical understanding of the organisation's impact, and this finds expression in the impact analysis report. Tuning thus takes place between the scored output, manifested as the rating, and the analytical understanding, as articulated in the report.

Both the report and the rating are passed from the analyst up to the internal impact committee for discussion and review, as well as being sent back past the organisation in question. This serves to check the accuracy of the report, but also to ensure that the rating and the analysis make sense together, and that the one can justify the other. If there is a repeat discrepancy, this in effect points toward an imbalance in the weightings, which can then be adjusted.

Obviously to be continuously rebalancing the weightings from one analysis to the next would introduce an intolerable level of inconsistency, and severely compromise the usefulness of the MIAA itself. Instead the purpose of assigning and tuning weights is to arrive at a set of weightings and stick with them. However, as the highly dynamic social-purpose universe continues to expand and develop, it is important to continue reviewing the results of analysis, and to review the weightings on an annual basis (indeed it is important to review also the methodology itself). While on one level this may seem to present a degree of potential inconsistency in the results, it is one that occurs at the margins of tuning (our experience has been that the weights of the major analytical blocks remain consistent, while adjustments occur around moving a point or two back and forth among considerations). More importantly, this level of reviewing does not compromise the deeper consistency of the analytical process, or the nature of the analytical understanding it gives rise to.

The Weighted Impact Scoresheet laid out here shows the weightings for the 56 scoring considerations that make up the MIAA Impact analysis. The actual spreadsheet used by a working analyst includes also the key questions relating to each consideration (i.e. those shown in the tables at the beginning of each of the three sections above — see 1. Mission Fulfilment, 2. Beneficiary Perspective, 3. Wider Impacts), and empty cells for the notes. These are not reproduced here simply to save space and fit the scoresheet onto one spread.

INVESTING FOR GOOD

#	IMPACT	POTENTIAL SCORE	SCORE AWARDED
1	**MISSION FULFILMENT**	**40**	
1.1	Mission Statement	2	
1.1.1	Mission Statement	2	
1.2	Context and Focus	3	
1.2.1	Understanding the Problem	2	
1.2.2	Understanding Beneficiaries	1	
1.3	Impact Activities	15	
1.3.1	Theory of Change	3	
1.3.2-a	Impact Measurement: Use of Appropriate Indicators	2	
1.3.2-b	Impact Measurement: Quality of Data	1	
1.3.2-c	Impact Measurement: Targets and Objectives	1	
1.3.3-a	Impact Reporting: Transparency	2	
1.3.3-b	Impact Reporting: External Validation	1	
1.3.4-a	Balance and Alignment: Congruence	3	
1.3.4-b	Balance and Alignment: Attitude to Profit	1	
1.3.4-c	Balance and Alignment: Mission Drift	1	
1.4	Results	12	
1.4.1-a	Results: Delivery of Impact	5	
1.4.1-b	Results: Targets and Objectives	2	
1.4.1-c	Results: Performance Improvement	2	
1.4.2-a	Accreditation and Comparison: Accreditation	1	
1.4.2-b	Accreditation and Comparison: Class Comparison	2	
1.5	Moving Forward	8	
1.5.1	Results Assessment and Response	3	
1.5.2	Planning and Strategy	2	
1.5.3-a	Sustainability and Growth: Sustainability of Impacts	1	
1.5.3-b	Sustainability and Growth: Future Growth	2	
2	**BENEFICIARY PERSPECTIVE**	**40**	
2.1	Beneficiary Focus	15	
2.1.2	Beneficiary Awareness, Access and Inclusion	2	
2.1.2	Beneficiary Consultation	4	
2.1.3	Beneficiary Empowerment	6	
2.1.4	Beneficiaries Connect	2	
2.1.5	Beneficiary Satisfaction	1	

THE GOOD ANALYST METHODOLOGY FOR IMPACT ANALYSIS AND ASSESSMENT (MIAA)

2.2	**Beneficiary Impacts**	**25**
2.2.1-a	Rights Matrix: Education and Family	4
2.2.1-b	Rights Matrix: Employment	4
2.2.1-c	Rights Matrix: Housing and Essential Needs	4
2.2.1-d	Rights Matrix: Economic Factors	4
2.2.1-e	Rights Matrix: Health	4
2.2.1-f	Rights Matrix: High Risk Behaviour	4
2.2.1-g	Rights Matrix: Care of Disabled and Older People	4
2.2.1-h	Rights Matrix: Safety and Community	4
2.2.1-i	Rights Matrix: Arts, Culture and Sports	4
2.2.1-j	Rights Matrix: Information, Understanding and Expression	4
2.2.1-k	Rights Matrix: Local Environment	4
2.2.1-l	Rights Matrix: Well-Being	4
2.2.1-m	Rights Matrix: Conservation and Biodiversity	4
2.2.1-n	Rights Matrix: Greenhouse Gas Emissions	4
2.2.1-o	Rights Matrix: Consumption, Waste, Pollution and Recycling	4
2.2.1-Σ	Rights Matrix: TOTAL	15*
2.2.2	Unit Cost	10†
3	**WIDER IMPACT**	**30**
3.1	**Additionality**	**8**
3.1.1	Impact over the BAU	4
3.1.2	Cost Benefits	4
3.2	**Impact Multipliers**	**12**
3.2.1-a	Economic Boost: Direct Spending	1
3.2.1-b	Economic Boost: Recirculation and New Spending	2
3.2.1-c	Economic Boost: Direct Investment	1
3.2.1-d	Economic Boost: Local Value	2
3.2.2-a	Knowledge Boost: Sharing Information Within the Sector	2
3.2.2-b	Knowledge Boost: Representation to Government and Business	2
3.2.2-c	Knowledge Boost: Raising Public Awareness	2
3.3	**Game Change**	**4**
3.3.1	Innovation of Approach	2
3.3.2	Pioneering of New Models	2
3.4	**Impact Risk**	**4**
3.4.1	Diversification of Impacts	2
3.4.2	Policy Dependency	2
3.5	**Responsible Management**	**2**
3.5.1	Responsible Management	2
ALL	**TOTAL**	**110**

INVESTING FOR GOOD

NOTES

* 2.2.1 Matrix of Human, Social and Environmental Rights and Benefits
A maximum of 4 points may be awarded to an organisation for major primary impacts within any individual field within the matrix. Secondary impacts on further fronts may score up to 2 points. When the organisation's impacts have been considered and assessed against the fifteen fields, the points awarded are added up to produce a total score up to a maximum of 15 (i.e. if an organisation has been awarded more than 15 points across the different fields, the maximum score of 15 is used).

N.B. It is possible for an organisation to be achieving primary impacts in more than one field. The distinction between primary and secondary impacts is between impacts that are generated directly and primarily by the organisation's activities (and are most likely a key aspect of its mission), and impacts that come about subsequently as a result of primary impacts resonating outwards through the lives of beneficiaries.

† 2.2.2 Unit Cost
A maximum of 10 points may be awarded to an organisation for the Unit Cost of its impact (representing the breadth of change achieved). However given current levels of available data and benchmarking, Unit Cost remains a relatively crude measure, and analysts are unlikely to be able to distinguish meaningfully between scores of e.g. 6, 7 and 7.5. Consequently it is more stable to score Unit Cost out of 3, and then multiply this score up to give the result out of 10, and so achieve the appropriate weight within the scoresheet.

BANDING

The final aggregated score translates into an Investing for Good rating of 1, 2 or 3. The bands for the ratings are as follows:

SCORE	RATING
75+	1
50–74	2
25-49	3
0–24	no rating

5. APPENDIX B: IMPACT OF CONTRIBUTION

Sections 1 to 3 considered the impact from the perspectives of the social-purpose organisation, the beneficiary and the wider context respectively, and constitute the full MIAA analysis of the organisation's impact. In some circumstances however a capital provider may further be interested in the impact of their own specific capital contribution (referred to as the "contribution"). In such cases an Impact of Contribution analysis can be applied as a MIAA bolt-on (for a more complete discussion of the use of the bolt-on and the grade it produces, see Part I, 3. MIAA: Development and Overview).

Rather than attempting to slice out a section or proportion of the impact of the organisation on beneficiaries, the capital provider's contribution is viewed in terms of how it has affected the organisation (and implicitly thereby the ability of the organisation to achieve impact). The essential question is: *What is the impact of the contribution on the social-purpose organisation?*

The assessment is divided into five sections:

   5.1 Scale of Contribution
   5.2 Leverage of Contribution
   5.3 Financial Management and Advice
   5.4 Growth Through Contribution
   5.5 Use of Contribution

The considerations that comprise the Impact of Contribution analysis are laid out and worked through over the following pages, succeeded by the summary table, which includes the weighted scores. As with the Impact assessment, where the totalled score produces a rating, totalling the scores of the Impact of Contribution assessment produces a grade. When the Impact of Contribution bolt-on is applied this grade accompanies the impact rating.

5.1 Scale of Contribution

How significant in terms of volume is the contribution with respect to the organisation's capitalisation or the project financing?

Scale of Contribution looks at the size of the contribution in comparison with the size of the social-purpose organisation. There are three key ratios:

> **i. size of contribution / current balance sheet total**
> This gives an indication of the significance of the contribution in comparison with the asset base of the organisation. If the organisation is looking to raise capital for a substantial new venture or expansion (e.g. opening a new branch of operations, buying a property), this ratio will suggest the comparative scale of the venture.
>
> **ii. size of contribution / total annual income**
> For contributions which provide working capital, this gives an indication of the significance of the contribution to the organisation's ongoing operations.
>
> **iii. size of contribution / total capital required for project**
> For contributions which provide capital for a specific project, this gives an indication of the significance of the contribution to the capitalisation of that project.

SCORING	
LOW	The contribution is small in comparison with the organisation and its projects, with a ratio of 0.5 or less on all three ratios.
MEDIUM	The contribution is small in relation to the organisation (a ratio of less than 0.5 on i.), but significant in comparison with the project — if for project capital — or the income — if for working capital (equating to a ratio more than 0.5 on ii. or iii.).
HIGH	The contribution is significant to the organisation and to the project — if for project capital — or the income — if for working capital (a ratio of 0.5 or more on two of i., ii. and iii.).

5.2 Leverage of Contribution
Does the contribution play a critical structural role in the organisation's capitalisation or the project financing?

The contribution may play a critical role in leveraging further financing from other providers, as occurs with, for example, matched funding or keystone investments. It may alternatively have an additional leveraging effect if it serves as a final-brick or needed bridge within an established financial structure, and so unlocks the rest of the committed capital. Typically this occurs with particular projects which have established but incomplete financing.

If the contribution instead supports the main working operations of the organisation, and the organisation is dependent upon this contribution (i.e. it would otherwise become unviable), the contribution can again be seen to have an enhanced effect. Financing which is central to the ongoing capacity of the organisation to exist can be seen to lever the rest of that organisation's impact.

An important aspect of the leverage of the contribution is the organisation's potential access to capital from other sources were this contribution not forthcoming. If the provider is clearly playing a unique role in making capital available to the organisation, then again it has additional leverage.

SCORING	
LOW	The organisation's financing is essentially independent of the contribution, and the organisation is likely to be able to access credit from other sources (or continue without it).
MEDIUM	The financial structure is arranged independent of the contribution, but the contribution plays an important role in capitalising that structure and ensuring other funds already committed or being committed are released and used.
HIGH	The contribution is an essential part of the core financial structure and serves to leverage further capital from other sources OR the contribution provides essential financing which the organisation would otherwise be unable to access (thus securing its ongoing financial health and ability to generate impact).

5.3 Financial Management and Advice

Does the contribution play a role in reshaping how the organisation manages its finances, and is additional financial advice and expertise being provided alongside the contribution?

Social-purpose organisations are often less familiar with investment and debt products than companies in the commercial sector, and may sometimes be less developed regarding their general accounting and financial discipline. The contribution may have implications in this regard (e.g. by imposing more exacting financial reporting requirements), which may in turn prove beneficial to the organisation on the operational level. Structuring an offering and taking on capital can, in this way, have a positive impact on the financial management of the organisation beyond the value of the raw capital input.

In some cases capital providers may also be providing financial and business advice. This may include helping structure financial products or offering advice around the use of credit (most obviously concerning the financial arrangement between the provider and the organisation), and may also cover operational aspects of financial planning and managing finances, as well as business advice. Where capital providers have relevant expertise, additional advisory services can enhance the relationship and the value of the contribution to the organisation.

Consideration is given to any improvements the organisation has made in its financial management as a result of the contribution and / or any advice or support given by the capital provider in this regard.

SCORING	
LOW	The contribution has no impact on the organisation's financial management practices, and there is no advisory relationship between the capital provider and the organisation.
MEDIUM	The contribution plays a significant role in the organisation improving its financial management and use of capital, but the capital provider has limited direct input OR the capital provider provides some useful financial advice and guidance and may help the organisation with the finer points of financial discipline. However the organisation is reasonably familiar with managing its finances and the changes are minor.
HIGH	The contribution and advice supplied with it by the capital provider play a leading role in helping the organisation reshape how it manages its finances and financial planning, and in how it thinks about accessing and using capital.

5.4 Growth Through Contribution
Does the contribution stimulate new growth?

Growth Through Contribution looks to the extent to which the contribution stimulates growth — less in the sense of a direct increase appearing on the balance sheet, and more in terms of growth in the organisation's operations and revenues. The contribution gains in significance if it allows the organisation to expand and pursue new activities that generate additional revenues, which are available in turn for being driven into further growth. This can be especially critical when the stimulated growth brings the organisation to a "break-even" or self-sustainable point. Contributions that unlock growth in this way serve to reduce the dependency of the organisation on external funding, free up future fundraising for impact-focused activities and growth (as opposed to working capital), and potentially "prove" the model and support longer-term and more strategic planning. All of this feeds into the scaling of the organisation's impact.

Consideration is given to the extent to which the contribution stimulates new growth, and the implications it has for operational viability and self-sustainability.

SCORING	
LOW	The contribution does not stimulate any particular new growth.
MEDIUM	The contribution frees up resources or funds activities directly in a way that allows the organisation to grow its activities and impact proportionally, but without unleashing any substantial new growth in operations or revenues OR the contribution does generate some growth and increased revenues, but these are small in comparison with turnover and do not have a significant impact on the organisation's self-sustainability.
HIGH	The contribution directly facilitates new projects and activities that generate revenues, fuelling organisational growth, and tipping the organisation into self-sustaining and scalable operations.

5.5 Use of Contribution (for reviews)
Is the contribution being used as intended — or for other impact-generating activities?

For contributions that have been placed already and are being reviewed (e.g. on an annual basis), it is relevant to ask if the contribution has been used — i.e. drawn down and actively deployed — and used for what it was originally intended for. The key points are:

- has the contribution been drawn down?
- has it been used for the proposed purposes?
- has the action plan been successful (i.e. the proposed purposes are progressing on time, in budget etc.)?
- has it served to improve impact?

It is possible that, due to shifting circumstances (e.g. changes in funding, changes in the policy environment), the original intended use is no longer the best or most appropriate use of the contribution. In such cases, organisations that are able to redeploy the capital flexibly into other more productive activities or aspects of their work, may equally be assessed to be using the contribution well. It rests with the organisation to make the case for the new use. The key points for assessment remain:

- the active use of capital
- a plan for its use, and indicators to show that the plan is progressing successfully
- direct evidence that — or a clear argument as to how — the plan is serving to grow the organisation's impact

SCORING	
LOW	The contribution either: has not been drawn down; remains in the bank or invested in non-mission related investments; has been drawn down and used but not for the proposed purpose, with inadequate justification, and in a way that is not generating impact.
MEDIUM	The contribution has been drawn down and used for the proposed purpose, but delays or complications may have impeded progress, and the improved impact is not fully forthcoming OR the contribution is being redeployed into new activities and for convincing reasons, but this has delayed progress.
HIGH	The contribution has been drawn down and the proposed purpose is progressing to plan, with the growth in impact forthcoming as anticipated OR the contribution has been drawn down and flexibly reapplied to a different purpose, with a clear line to growth in impact delivery.

Impact of Contribution Assessment Table

5	IMPACT OF CONTRIBUTION	POTENTIAL SCORE	SCORE AWARDED
5.1	**Scale of Contribution**		
	How significant in terms of volume is the contribution with respect to the organisation's capitalisation or the project financing?	5	
5.2	**Leverage of Contribution**		
	Does the contribution play a critical structural role in the organisation's capitalisation or the project financing?	3	
5.3	**Financial Management and Advice**		
	Does the contribution play a role in reshaping how the organisation manages its finances, and is additional financial advice and expertise being provided alongside the contribution?	3	
5.4	**Growth Through Contribution**		
	Does the contribution stimulate new growth?	4	
5.5	**Use of Contribution (for reviews)**		
	Is the contribution being used as intended — or for other impact-generating activities?	5*	
ALL	**TOTAL**	20	

INVESTING FOR GOOD

NOTES

* The Use of Contribution assessment can only be applied to contributions that have already been made and are being reviewed. If the contribution under analysis is new then this consideration is skipped, and the points redistributed across the other four considerations proportionally (i.e. the first four considerations become worth 7, 4, 4 and 5 respectively).

BANDING

The final aggregated score translates into an Impact of Contribution grade of A, B or C. This grade accompanies the impact rating (see Part I, 3. MIAA: Development and Overview).

The bands for the grades are as follows:

SCORE	RATING
15+	A
8–14	B
0–7	C

6. APPENDIX C: BENEFICIARY PERSPECTIVE INDICATOR TABLES

The Beneficiary Perspective Indicator Tables serve chiefly to support the analyst in assessing the section 2.2.1 Matrix of Human, Social and Environmental Rights and Benefits. The tables do not aim to set out an exhaustive list of all possible forms of impact and associated indicators (nor do they imply then scrutinising organisations against such a list for compliance). Rather they act as a reference tool, providing the analyst with research information regarding the main areas of focus and key points that typically are pertinent to each of the fifteen fields of rights and benefits that make up the matrix. By setting out what may be at stake in relation to a particular right, a table can throw into relief the benefits being achieved in that area, and give greater depth and definition to the analysis.

The tables also cover section 2.1 Beneficiary Focus with the same approach and purpose.

The Appendix thus comprises:

6.1 Indicator Tables for 2.1 Beneficiary Focus
(covering: 2.1.1 Beneficiary Awareness, Access and Inclusion; 2.1.2 Beneficiary Consultation; 2.1.3 Beneficiary Empowerment; 2.1.4 Beneficiaries Connect; 2.1.5 Beneficiary Satisfaction)

6.2 Indicator Tables for 2.2.1 Matrix of Human, Social and Environmental Rights and Benefits
(covering: a. Education and Family; b. Employment; c. Housing and Essential Needs; d. Economic Factors; e. Health; f. High Risk Behaviour; g. Care of Disabled and Older People; h. Safety and Community; i. Arts, Culture and Sports; j. Information, Understanding and Expression; k. Local Environment; l. Well-Being; m. Conservation and Biodiversity; n. Greenhouse Gas Emissions; o. Consumption, Waste, Pollution and Recycling)

6.1 Indicator Tables for 2.1 Beneficiary Focus

2.1.1 BENEFICIARY AWARENESS, ACCESS AND INCLUSION

FOCUS	POINT	POTENTIAL INDICATORS
beneficiary awareness of organisation and its services	beneficiaries are aware of the organisation and the services and spaces it offers beneficiaries are aware of their own situation and needs	number and proportion of target population aware of organisation and its services (shown through e.g. awareness surveys) distribution of information about services (e.g. newsletters, publications, website, hotline, use of community resources to propagate word of mouth) number of website hits, downloads, calls to hotline number of pieces published in the media associated with the organisation's work number of enquiries, applications for services
access of services	beneficiaries are able to access services with respect to: • transport • disabled access • communication (language) • financial barriers uptake of services is not limited by access issues services provided are ones which beneficiaries are otherwise unable to access	number of beneficiaries receiving services number of potential beneficiaries turned away or finding barriers to entry number of other organisations accessible to target population offering similar services
inclusion	organisation's outreach is inclusive, representative, and diverse awareness and access reaches minority and disadvantaged groups benefits of services are representative and inclusive	information showing uptake of services is representative and inclusive (beneficiaries are representative of the target population, e.g. with respect to gender, ethnic minorities, disadvantaged groups) information showing successful outcomes and participation in programmes are representative and inclusive (i.e. particular groups, e.g. women, do equally well from services as others) number of previously excluded people now accessing services

2.1.2 BENEFICIARY CONSULTATION

FOCUS	POINT	POTENTIAL INDICATORS
beneficiaries are informed	beneficiaries understand the organisation's services and what it aims to achieve	transparent information made available to beneficiaries (uptake)
	beneficiaries are informed of results (in a meaningful format)	
beneficiary consultation	beneficiaries are able to communicate and express their views on activities and on their own progress	use of surveys, questionnaires, interviews, discussion groups procedures for beneficiary feedback (comments, suggestions, complaints)
	beneficiaries share their knowledge with the organisation	
choice	beneficiaries are able to make informed choices about which services and forms of support will best meet their needs	number of choices offered to beneficiaries
consultation influences planning	beneficiary consultation supports activities, feeds into planning and decision-making	incorporation of consultation (in some form) into impact measurement system

2.1.3 BENEFICIARY EMPOWERMENT

FOCUS	POINT	POTENTIAL INDICATORS
beneficiary participation in activities	beneficiaries are supported with the understanding, confidence and skills needed to participate	number of beneficiaries supported to become more actively involved in decision making regarding their support
	beneficiaries are involved with service planning / design	number of involvement groups / participation sessions run (beneficiary attendance)
	results are shared with beneficiaries including feedback and review of involvement	number participating in planning, design and delivery of services and activities; number of user-run activities taking place

INVESTING FOR GOOD

beneficiary use of invested capital	beneficiaries are able to influence the use of invested capital through engagement with the organisation's processes	decisions made regarding use of capital with beneficiary input
	beneficiaries access invested capital themselves through credit	volume of capital lent to beneficiaries
beneficiaries define impact	beneficiaries participate in setting of goals and selection of indicators	impact assessment groups held with beneficiaries
	beneficiaries test surveys, questionnaires etc.	indicators / measurement tools developed with beneficiary input
beneficiary roles with organisation	volunteering	number of beneficiaries taking positions within the organisation and beginning to give support to others
	employment within the organisation (e.g. providing support, training staff)	participation in public meetings, meetings with policy-makers etc.
	engagement with advocacy (expressing beneficiary perspective to external bodies)	changes in public attitudes or policy influenced by beneficiary advocacy
	inclusion of beneficiaries on boards (or in appointing boards members)	length of time role of beneficiaries is sustained
	beneficiary ownership of organisation (e.g. through shares, cooperatives structures)	
	beneficiary role is sustained over time	
beneficiary empowerment	beneficiaries feel they can make a difference (to their own lives, to the services they use, to others)	beneficiaries report feeling empowered

2.1.4 BENEFICIARIES CONNECT

FOCUS	POINT	POTENTIAL INDICATORS
facilitate beneficiary communication building beneficiary groups and social networks	organisation uses services to leverage social interaction among beneficiaries (promotes links to community, networks, groups for beneficiaries) organisation's work supports / helps build social networks with family, friends, support workers sharing of information, understanding, skills, experience among beneficiaries	number of beneficiaries supported to develop positive new relationships / friendships number supported to build / strengthen relationships with family members number supported to develop parenting and caring roles number supported to begin accessing peer support or self-help groups

2.1.5 BENEFICIARY SATISFACTION

FOCUS	POINT	POTENTIAL INDICATORS
beneficiary satisfaction	evidence of beneficiary satisfaction	beneficiaries report that services are responsive to their needs beneficiaries report that services help them achieve their personal goals retention rate of beneficiaries (ongoing service provision) boost in demand number of new users referred to organisation by existing beneficiaries

INVESTING FOR GOOD

6.2 Indicator Tables for 2.2.1 Matrix of Human, Social and Environmental Rights and Benefits

A. EDUCATION AND FAMILY

Impacts advance beneficiary access to the right to education and the right to enjoy family life in a safe and supportive environment. covers: education, parents, child and youth needs and basic care, marital and family support, women and domestic abuse

EDUCATION

FOCUS	POINT	POTENTIAL INDICATORS
education	provision of traditional (academic) education services	number of beneficiaries enrolled in education programme
		attendance at education programme
		pupil-hours of schooling delivered
		tangible educational gains (standards met, levels passed, qualifications)
		number reaching expected national standard for literacy and numeracy for their schooling level
		number reintroduced to mainstream schooling (having been excluded)
		number advancing (from one level of schooling to the next, finishing school)
		number enrolling in further education
		number establishing employment, career
		number of days absent from school (truanting)
		number of days excluded from school
		parent-teacher engagement (see **parents** below)

extracurricular programmes and activities	provision of extracurricular (non-conventional schooling) programmes and activities (e.g. arts, sports, community services)	number enrolled in programme attendance at programme improved behaviour (see **child and youth needs and basic care** below) improved academic achievement / performance on tests number reintroduced to mainstream schooling (having been excluded) number advancing (from one level of schooling to the next, finishing school) number enrolling in further education number establishing employment, career
youth offending	reduction in youth offending	contact with criminal justice system (crimes committed) severity of crimes committed numbers of crimes committed levels of anti- and pro-social behaviour levels of involvement in gangs use of drugs and alcohol
understanding progress	self-reports of beneficiaries improved beneficiary well-being	improved attitudes and motivation decreased levels of anger / alienation improved self-worth / self-esteem feeling good about yourself improved relationships with family members (see **I. Well-Being**)

INVESTING FOR GOOD

PARENTS

FOCUS	POINT	POTENTIAL INDICATORS
childcare and support for parents	childcare	hours of childcare provided
	programmes for parents (education, guidance, advice)	improved parental awareness (see **child and youth needs and basic care** below)
parental involvement	parental involvement in groups, education, activities for children	number of parents attending groups
		number contributing to groups, leading activities
		number of partnerships formed with parents (parents design and implement activities)
		number of parents on organisation's board
		parents report feeling confident that their contributions to parenting groups will be taken seriously by group leaders
		number of parents advocating for community support (see **j. Information, Understanding, Expression**)
families with children with special needs	advice for families with children with special needs	number of consultations with families / advice given
	programmes and activities for children with special needs	number of children with special needs entering programmes / activities
	respite for families, carers	respite provision for families (hours / days respite)
		parents report reduced stress from caring for child with special needs

CHILD AND YOUTH NEEDS AND BASIC CARE (see also l. Well-Being)

FOCUS	POINT	POTENTIAL INDICATORS
basic care	ensuring safety	number of accidents (reduction)
		number of violent incidents at home (reduction)
		number of violent incidents outside the home (reduction)

physical health	levels of child nutrition
	routine medical examinations observed
	measures of child health
behaviour	levels of negative, challenging or inappropriate behaviour (frequency, duration, intensity)
	number of non-age appropriate tantrums
	incidences of self-destructive or suicidal behaviour
	involvement in bullying (number of incidents)
	suffering from bullying (number of incidents)
	levels of disorganisation, inattentiveness (observed)
	uses positive methods to initiate interactions with others (observed)
	expresses needs in appropriate ways (observed)
	levels of self-care skills
citizenship	youth offending, antisocial behaviour (see **youth offending** above)
supporting learning	school, attendance, development (see **education** above)
social networks	number of friends
	quality of friends (friends you can trust)
	feeling lonely or isolated
	number of relationships with key adults (role models)
family relationships	parents and children report appropriate structures and boundaries in place
	parents and children report on the keeping of a routine
	parents and children report on meaningful use of time
	parents and children report on meeting of emotional needs
	parents and children report on how happy the home is
	parents and children report on feelings of control

| | family stability | number of families in stable long term housing
household income
level of social integration (family reports feeling a part of the community, see **h. Safety and Community**) |

MARITAL AND FAMILY SUPPORT

FOCUS	POINT	POTENTIAL INDICATORS
marriage and family support (family breakdown)	marriage guidance and counselling relationship guidance and counselling	number of couples receiving counselling number (proportion) of families in crisis who resolve their issues (and identify support services as contributing factor) family members report satisfaction with support services

WOMEN AND DOMESTIC ABUSE

FOCUS	POINT	POTENTIAL INDICATORS
women and families subject to domestic abuse	provision of support for women suffering domestic abuse	number of women accessing support number of incidences of domestic violence (change in number) level of violence (numbers of incidents resulting in GP consultations, visits to A&E, hospital stays) reported level of satisfaction with police response to domestic violence level of self-harming number of children on the Child Protection Register (change in number)
	provision of alternative housing for women suffering domestic abuse	number of women finding a place of safety in a women's refuge number of women who were previously in a violent domestic situation now living in a safe and stable environment (see **c. Housing and Essential Needs**)

THE GOOD ANALYST METHODOLOGY FOR IMPACT ANALYSIS AND ASSESSMENT (MIAA)

B. EMPLOYMENT

Impacts advance beneficiary access to the right to employment.
covers: employment, training and advice, support for professional advancement

EMPLOYMENT		
FOCUS	POINT	POTENTIAL INDICATORS
development of skills and training	provision of personal / life skills development programmes (soft skills)	number of beneficiaries enrolling in programme (attendance)
	provision of employment-orientated training programmes (hard skills)	number (proportion) completing programme (drop-off)
	provision of advice, mentoring	number (proportion) passing job skills competency tests after completing training; gaining a meaningful qualification
	expansion of social and professional networks	number (proportion) enrolling in further education or occupational skills training programmes
		number reporting satisfaction with training / advice
		number connected with each other regarding employment (expansion of social and professional networks)
		number accessing advice about employment
		number (proportion) gaining employment (see **find jobs** below)
		number (proportion) making progress toward employment (see **understanding progress toward employment** below)
find jobs	encourage beneficiaries to apply for and find jobs	number of people previously disadvantaged or excluded from employment (e.g. NEETs, homeless people, disabled people) now in paid employment
	provision of jobs through employer partners	• part time (under 16 hours a week)
	creation of jobs directly within organisation	• full time (over 16 hours a week)
		wage levels (address of: comparable wage, wage growth, wage equity within employer organisation)
		employment package (address of: leave, benefits, support, opportunities for training, employee representation etc.)
		number entering into voluntary work placements
		number becoming self-employed

understanding progress toward employment		number of applications for paid employment
		number of job interviews attended
		number gaining a job within x months of programme completion / contact with organisation
		number of employer partners
		number of jobs offered by employer partners
		number of repeat hires by employer partners
		number staying in job for 6 months or more
		number who remain employed after 12 months
		beneficiaries report satisfaction with job (meeting of expectations)
		beneficiaries attribute job to support of organisation
	aspects of progress observable through monitoring and / or self-reports	Aspiration and motivation • hope • sense of direction • energy • initiative • willingness to make changes • accepting responsibility for development (see also **I. Well-Being**)
		Stability • issues with drugs or alcohol • insecure housing, problems with debt, or other issues that might affect employment • eating, sleeping, hygiene • health • engagement with structured activities • self-control • reliability • planning and organising • ability to manage money

Basic skills	Social skills for work	Work skills
• English • literacy • numeracy • IT • use of telephone • ability to deal with forms • completion of CV	• getting on with people • self-confidence • turning up on time • behaving appropriately • working with teams • presentation and appearance • phone manner • interview skills • dealing with authority • assertiveness	• job-specific training • ability to learn and continue learning • ability to reason • ability to problem-solve • ability to prioritise effectively

| economic benefits | increased income for beneficiaries (enhanced economic well-being, self-sufficiency) savings for government | increased earnings of beneficiaries number attaining economic stability 12 months after programme / contact with organisation; 2 years after programme / contact with organisation number of individuals moving off benefits (e.g. income support, housing benefit etc.) and into employment subsequent to completion of programme / contact with organisation (financial value of undrawn benefits) increase in tax revenues from jobs created local productivity growth beneficiaries report increased financial security see also **d. Economic Factors** |

C. HOUSING AND ESSENTIAL NEEDS

Impacts advance beneficiary access to the right to housing within a healthy and sustainable environment, and the right to adequate provisions regarding domestic and home needs.
covers: housing and essential needs

HOUSING AND ESSENTIAL NEEDS

FOCUS	POINT	POTENTIAL INDICATORS
shelter needs	meet immediate shelter needs (beneficiaries may include: homeless people, unemployed people, people with mental health needs, disabled people, poor widows and single women, young families, prison leavers (ex-offenders), people with substance abuse issues / issues with addiction)	number of bed-nights provided (percent capacity of shelter) number of unique beneficiaries using shelter (number re-entering) number applying to shelter change in number of people sleeping rough number (proportion) of beneficiaries who remain in the shelter three or more days and utilize services (see **support / additional services** below)
	meet intermediate and long term shelter and housing needs	number (proportion) of beneficiaries applying to transitional housing number (proportion) who move to a transitional shelter, a rehabilitative setting (excluding prison), or the home of a friend or family member (intermediate shelter needs met) number (proportion) who move to safe permanent housing number who maintain safe and stable housing for six consecutive months after leaving the shelter number who do not re-enter the homeless system within one year of obtaining permanent housing (long term need met)
support / additional services	provision of support and additional services	number (proportion) of beneficiaries who develop a service / treatment plan (after x days at shelter) number who complete service / treatment plan number who participate in referral programs number who participate in planning and delivery of support services

	services relating to physical and mental health	number of beneficiaries who register and attend GP services number who register and attend mental health / counselling support services number who obtain / maintain routine medical examinations number who know when it is appropriate to seek medical care (see **e. Health**)
	services relating to addiction	number of beneficiaries who register and attend drug / alcohol / addiction rehabilitation services (see **f. High Risk Behaviour**)
	services relating to management of finances	number of beneficiaries who receive financial advice number who begin to access income support (see **d. Economic Factors**)
	services relating to employment	number of beneficiaries who register and attend education, training and employment services (see **b. Employment**)
affordable housing and tenancy issues	increase supply of affordable housing	number of new housing units built / made available change in number (proportion) of target population with access to affordable housing
	increase uptake of affordable housing	number of beneficiaries supported to secure affordable long term housing conditions of home environment (state of repair, appropriate for needs)
	improvements in behaviour by tenants	managing tenancy (issues with rent, opening post, dealing with forms, bills etc., relations with other residents) taking care of housing, making repairs reduced incidence of antisocial behaviour number of beneficiaries supported to manage relationships with neighbours
	changes in the likelihood of eviction	number of beneficiaries supported to resolve issues with their landlords number supported to manage finances and meet arrears number (change) of evictions

INVESTING FOR GOOD

	improve resident safety, maintenance and quality of local environment	number and rate of crimes
		residents report feeling safe
		residents report satisfaction with condition of housing units
		residents report satisfaction with maintenance of housing and local environment
		numbers of complaints received, resolved
		turnover of residents, vacancy
		access to greenspace
		new investment in area
		(see **h. Safety and Community**)
supported accommodation	support stable and long term accommodation solutions	number of beneficiaries supported to move to more independent accommodation
		number supported to move to more suitable (but not more independent) accommodation
		number supported to obtain safe and affordable housing
living skills: domestic	support development of domestic living skills	number of beneficiaries supported to develop new skills for (more) independent living (e.g. cooking, shopping for food, looking after self)
		number supported to begin leaving the house; using public transport independently; enjoying mobility and being able to get around
		number who are able to access help in an emergency

D. ECONOMIC FACTORS

Impacts advance beneficiary access to rights to economic means and security.
covers: access to financial services, financial security, financial management

ECONOMIC FACTORS

FOCUS	POINT	POTENTIAL INDICATORS
financial services for individuals	access to financial services: • credit • debt advice • savings • insurance • financial literacy	uptake of credit facilities (decrease in number of individuals using doorstep lenders) average loan size (purpose of borrowing); loan delinquency rate number of bank accounts, insurance policies held by those who previously did not qualify increase in individual or household savings number of people accessing financial advice (money management, financial literacy)
financial services for local businesses	access to financial services: • credit • training and advice • financial literacy	number of businesses (SMEs, social enterprises) provided with assistance or training number who began / expanded business within 12 months of assistance or training (and attributed new business operations at least in part to assistance) number still in business two years later change in number of businesses operating in area change in size and scale (turnover) of businesses number of businesses achieving sustainable growth increase in local employment

THE GOOD ANALYST METHODOLOGY FOR IMPACT ANALYSIS AND ASSESSMENT (MIAA)

financial security	greater beneficiary financial security	beneficiaries report feeling more financially secure
		levels of income, savings, debt
		beneficiaries have enough money to meet basic needs
	beneficiaries empowered to use and make decisions regarding money	measures of local level of economic deprivation
		• borough's position on the Index of Multiple Deprivation (IMD)
		• proportion of families on incomes of less than 60% of the median income
		• proportion of children living in poverty
		• incidence of fuel poverty
		• total value of household debt
		levels of local employment (unemployment)
		levels of anti-poverty benefits uptake
		number of individuals moving off benefits (e.g. income support, housing benefit, passported benefits such as free prescriptions)
		increase in individual / household income
living skills: financial	support development of financial stability and self-management	number of beneficiaries supported to manage their own finances effectively (accounts, forms, personal administration, household budget etc.)
		number supported to address and reduce a debt problem
		number supported to begin accessing state benefits (e.g. income support)

E. HEALTH

Impacts advance beneficiary access to the right to the highest attainable standard of physical and mental health. covers: health services, health education and the promotion of healthy lifestyles

HEALTH

FOCUS	POINT	POTENTIAL INDICATORS
medical / health service delivery	health services provided	number of: • patients seen / consultations • procedures / surgeries completed • drug treatments / immunisations administered • counselling / support sessions provided • patient beds provided number (proportion) of successful interventions (improvement of condition that was present upon referral to the organisation)
communication and recovery	improvements in health	[appropriate condition-specific indicators] beneficiary self-reports on improvements in health beneficiary satisfaction with health services and state of health (needs met) number of beneficiaries able to: • return to work • live at home (or other preferred environment) • be mobile • engage in recreation and other activities
	increase in beneficiary control and independence	number of beneficiaries provided with information to make choices number supported to become positively involved in decisions about their medication or treatment, and to develop a recovery plan number supported to develop and begin using new coping strategies number supported to decrease their reliance on medical services

health education and high risk behaviour	promoting awareness	number of awareness events, groups, meetings etc. organised by the organisation
number of people participating / exposed
number of pieces published in the media associated with the organisation's work
awareness levels among target beneficiaries (and influence of organisation) (see **j. Information, Understanding, Expression**)
	engaging purposefully with people	number of people showing increased knowledge about health issues and risk behaviour
increase in uptake of healthy practices (decrease in high risk behaviour)
number of people showing improved health / are healthy after 6 months, a year
number who report feeling healthier
reduction in incidence of associated health problems
healthy lifestyle	promoting healthy lifestyle	levels among beneficiaries of:
• smoking
• obesity
• drug use
• healthy diet, nutrition
• hours of physical exercise
• use of medical services, visits to GP etc.
• use of medications
• frequency of illnesses

F. HIGH RISK BEHAVIOUR

Impacts help beneficiaries manage high risk behaviour.
covers: offenders and ex-offenders, youth offending, substance abuse

OFFENDERS AND EX-OFFENDERS

FOCUS	POINT	POTENTIAL INDICATORS
offences	monitor levels of offences	numbers of crimes committed severity of crimes committed number of breaches of statutory orders contact with criminal justice system levels of anti- and pro-social behaviour rate of recidivism
support services	provision of support services programmes may cover: • housing • substance abuse • mental health issues • education and training	number of beneficiaries who develop a service plan (attendance) number who complete plan number with appropriate housing after release (see **c. Housing and Essential Needs**) number connected to local services after release (GP etc.) number abusing alcohol, drugs after release (see **substance abuse** below) number with mental health issues receiving appropriate support (see **e. Health**) number enrolled in education and training (attendance) (see **b. Employment**) number participating in job placement activity number finding employment number retaining employment 12 months after release

rehabilitation	monitor long term success of offenders after release	number (proportion) of beneficiaries who are law-abiding self-sufficient citizens after 12 months number who are law-abiding supported citizens after 12 months number who return to prison within 12 months number charged with misdemeanour offences number convicted of serious violent crime number re-entering programme number with mental health issues who are able to manage and remain free of psychiatric hospitalisations 12 months after release improvements to public safety (reduced crime in area, see **h. Community and Safety**)
family	reconnection of offenders and ex-offenders with family, significant others	number of beneficiaries supported to reunite with family, significant others number who report improved relations with family, significant others number supported to take on parenting roles and responsibilities number who report benefitting from increased family support

YOUTH OFFENDING

FOCUS	POINT	POTENTIAL INDICATORS
youth offending	reduction in youth offending	contact with criminal justice system (crimes committed) severity of crimes committed numbers of crimes committed levels of anti- and pro-social behaviour levels of involvement in gangs use of drugs and alcohol

SUBSTANCE ABUSE

FOCUS	POINT	POTENTIAL INDICATORS
alcohol abuse	monitor level and severity of alcohol abuse.	units of alcohol consumed days of alcohol usage in the past month amount of alcohol consumed on a typical day in the last month (self-reported) level of alcohol dependence number of A&E admissions due to alcohol incidence of alcoholism related illnesses
drug abuse	monitor level and severity of drug abuse	amount of drugs consumed days of drugs usage in the past month number of drug overdoses in the past month level of drug dependence use of drugs by injection use of needle or syringe which has been used by someone else / use of clean needle, syringe number of needles the public is exposed to number of drug users replacing heroin or crack use with methadone
support	provision of support programme	number of beneficiaries who develop a service plan / enrol in support programme (attendance) number who complete plan / programme number (proportion) of beneficiaries re-entering programme amount of counselling provided number of drug / alcohol dependent people who were using emergency services that are now no longer dependent on emergency services thanks to support programmes reduction in level and severity of drug / alcohol abuse number of lapses into abuse change in levels of unsafe drinking / drug abuse in area

G. CARE OF DISABLED AND OLDER PEOPLE

Impacts advance the access of disabled and older people to the right to a healthy and fulfilling life and the right to be as independently capable as possible.

covers: disabled people, older people

DISABLED PEOPLE

FOCUS	POINT	POTENTIAL INDICATORS
provision of services	services for disabled people	services may include: • housing / supported accommodation • meals • health care assistance • personal care • housekeeping assistance • specialist living equipment • fitness activities • transportation services • recreation activities • educational / cognitive activities • counselling / therapy • supported employment number of individuals applying number receiving services number enabled to live in an environment conducive to well being number supported to engage in independent living
life enhancements	support for improved beneficiary capabilities increase in beneficiary control	number of beneficiaries engaging in employment, training, voluntary activities number enjoying enhanced mobility number enabled to make more decisions about their lives see **I. Well-Being**

OLDER PEOPLE

FOCUS	POINT	POTENTIAL INDICATORS
home and safety	improve the homes and safety of older people	number of beneficiaries who are able to remain in their home thanks to support provided (who otherwise were likely to have had to give up their home / go into care) number enjoying improvements made to their homes as a result of aids, adaptations, home repairs and maintenance carried out through the organisation number (reduction) suffering accidents in their living environments number who report feeling happier with their home / have the kind of living environment that they want number who report feeling safe (for housing of older people, see **c. Housing and Essential Needs**)
control	support older people to maintain control	number of beneficiaries supported to be as independent as possible number supported to retain control over their support
health and activities	support older people to take part in activities and engage with others support older people to stay as well as they can	number of beneficiaries taking part in regular activities number taking regular exercise number keeping in touch with other people through activities number who report feeling more active and less isolated

INVESTING FOR GOOD

H. SAFETY AND COMMUNITY

Impacts advance beneficiary access to the right to a sense of community, and the right to personal safety and freedom from discrimination. covers: community, safety and crime

SAFETY AND COMMUNITY

FOCUS	POTENTIAL INDICATORS
perceptions of community and neighbourhood	people feel part of the community and a sense of belonging people are satisfied with their neighbourhood as a place to live / enjoy living here people feel the neighbourhood is improving (is getting worse)
social networks, community cohesion, social capital	people feel strong community cohesion people feel that individuals in their local area help one another people from different social, economic and cultural backgrounds spend time together and get on well people from different generations spend time together and get on well people know people locally people feel high levels of trust in neighbours people go out and meet other residents people feel the community is friendly people have strong social networks of friends, family and neighbours • speak to friends / neighbours / relatives at least once a week • have at least one close friend / relative who lives nearby • have people you can turn to when needing help (e.g. needing help when ill in bed, needing to borrow money) proportion of people who have helped or been helped by others (unpaid and not relatives) over the last year economic and cultural mix of communities (ghettoisation) economic and cultural diversity of intake of local services (e.g. schools)

THE GOOD ANALYST METHODOLOGY FOR IMPACT ANALYSIS AND ASSESSMENT (MIAA)

safety and crime	people feel safe (reduced levels of fear)
	people feel they can trust people living in their area
	people feel they can trust unfamiliar others
	people feel they can walk out at night
	local area is safe and well kept
	• levels of crime, antisocial behaviour, accidents
	• levels of vandalism, drunk and rowdy behaviour
	• levels of graffiti
	• level of victimisation (e.g. as recorded by the British Crime Survey)
	• perception of local crime level
	proportion of people who have been a victim of crime in the last 12 months
	number of accidents

I. ARTS, CULTURE, SPORTS

Impacts advance beneficiary access to the right to participation in cultural life including arts and sports. covers: arts and culture, sports and recreation

ARTS AND CULTURE

FOCUS	POINT	POTENTIAL INDICATORS
arts in the community	increased knowledge and appreciation of arts and culture life enriched community members pursue arts further enhanced community inclusion, cohesion	number of shows, performances attendance (number of people, average, percent capacity) number of artists supported reports of appreciation / satisfaction regarding arts arts programmes receive external recognition (critic reviews, awards etc.)
appreciation of local culture	local culture explored through art shows, performances	increased awareness of history of community
participation of community members in the arts / outreach services	community arts programmes offered (may include: education, outreach to disadvantaged community members) partnerships between arts groups and community organisations	number of education / outreach programmes run (attendance) improved community quality of life (see **h. Safety and Community**)

SPORTS AND RECREATION

FOCUS	POINT	POTENTIAL INDICATORS
sports in the community	provision of sport facilities, sports programmes, classes (dance, yoga, etc.) building healthier lifestyles, healthier communities	number of users / participants improved awareness of benefits of exercise health measures (rates of disease, obesity etc.)
outreach services	education / outreach programmes to disadvantaged or at risk members of the community through sports	number of users / participants reports of improved outlook, reduced anxiety, stress, depression (thanks to outlet through sports) reduced truanting, antisocial behaviour (see **a. Education and Family**) improved educational outcomes (sports as a hook to learning, team-work etc.) reduced crime rates (see **f. High Risk Behaviour**) enhanced community inclusion (improved relations between young people) improved community quality of life (see **h. Safety and Community**)

J. INFORMATION, UNDERSTANDING, EXPRESSION

Impacts advance beneficiary access to information and understanding regarding the issues under address, and access to the right to expression.

covers: communication within sector, advocacy, beneficiary expression, public awareness

INFORMATION, UNDERSTANDING, EXPRESSION

FOCUS	POINT	POTENTIAL INDICATORS
communication and information-sharing with sector	organisation shares information with sector and external bodies (e.g. on funding, legal matters, financial guidance, new research, impact reporting)	distribution of information (number of publications, reports, research papers, website hits, downloads, calls etc.) communications / agreements / partnerships formed with other organisations
	organisation's approach and results are published and made available to funders, beneficiaries and other sector organisations	
	research on beneficiary needs or approaches / techniques of other organisations performed and made available	
	evidence of good practice is shared with the wider community	
	techniques for good practice are sought from the wider community	

network activities	foster interest networks for community groups / sector organisations participate / facilitate: • events • conferences • meetings • focus groups support organisations to make links with other organisations, agencies and bodies integrate knowledge from across different groups and organisations and use it to leverage value from diverse sets of activities, including: • sharing of information, expertise • sharing of approaches, techniques, good practice • sharing of resources, facilities, equipment • cross-referral of service users (from one group or organisation to another they may benefit from) • promotion of new groups and organisations	number of networking events, conferences organised / attended (feedback from participating organisations) number of organisations brought together, networks formed number of new initiatives, collaborations, networks, partnerships formed number of service users referred between organisations number of new organisations formed

support the development of groups and organisations	support organisations with regard to: • financial barriers • needs for equipment • specialist professional advice (knowledge of processes, resources, policies, skills needed) provision of resources (project space, office space, office services etc.; see **local economy** below) promotion of new groups and organisations	number of new organisations and projects developed using the support organisation's resources and services new services provided by the new organisations uptake of new services (number of community members accessing services)
advocacy, leveraging political support	feed information up to policy-makers and planning bodies lobbying external bodies involved in planning and policy development (driven by understanding of needs) involvement with policy-making, policy review, local planning structures participation in research commissioned by relevant bodies, writing of guidance documents foster working agreements feed information from policy-makers to the sector	changes in policy, local planning, regulations (measures passed / development or changes in regulations related to the organisation's mission) number of policy or guidance documents published with contributions from or references to organisation references to organisation in policy statements, resolutions number of strategic partnerships formed new funding / donations / non-financial inputs leveraged

increase opportunities for beneficiary expression and participation in planning	organisation of meetings, events, opportunities for beneficiary participation and community engagement support beneficiaries with the knowledge and skills to become involved and to have an effective influence on policy-making	number of beneficiaries participating e.g. in public meetings number of elected representatives and policy makers engaging with beneficiary community changes in policy and public structures achieved with beneficiary input beneficiaries gain more control over resources, assets and services
increase public awareness, education and support	provision of information to public on organisation's core issues raising public awareness and support engaging with public opinion, public attitudes generating publicity and raising media presence garner high profile support (public support of issue from elected officials and well-known individuals) leverage additional resources (offers of funding, offers of non-financial inputs)	distribution of information (numbers of publications, website hits, downloads, calls to hotline, use of community resources to promote word of mouth) number of pieces published in the media associated with the organisation's work number of high-profile people individuals (e.g. elected officials, celebrities) engaging with organisation's mission number of people directly exposed to events, campaigns, message increase in public awareness; people report a positive attitude toward issue (issue becomes less stigmatised) value of funding leveraged value of non-financial inputs leveraged
increase public participation	organisation of meetings, events, opportunities for public participation and engagement	number of people participating

K. LOCAL ENVIRONMENT

Impacts advance beneficiary access to the right to live in a healthy and sustainable local environment with adequate infrastructure and community space.

covers: quality of locality, local community buildings, local infrastructure, transport

LOCAL ENVIRONMENT

FOCUS	POINT	POTENTIAL INDICATORS
quality of local environment	improve cleanliness, aesthetics of local environment (e.g. litter, detritus, weeds, fly-tipping, fly-posting, graffiti, dog-fouling, physical appearance and maintenance)	area of open space, public space number of people using public space / spending time outside number of people participating in ongoing maintenance of local environment reduction in litter etc. levels
	increase amount of local green space / public space (land e.g. freed up, rehabilitated, secured, purchased)	increase in property prices reduction in crime levels, reduction in reported fear of crime increase in reported satisfaction with local area improved community quality of life (see **h. Safety and Community**)
buildings	construction / renovation / purchase of community building	volume of new community space increase in value of community assets
	new / enhanced space for community use	
infrastructure	foster infrastructure developments, investment in infrastructure	volume of new infrastructure
transport	enhance local public transport (esp. to local essential services, community facilities)	increased use of public transport, reduced traffic, car road miles number of public transport users who previously had no access number of public transport users who previously used a car

L. WELL-BEING

Impacts advance the right to well-being.
covers: confidence, being able, being satisfied, feeling connected

WELL-BEING

FOCUS	POTENTIAL INDICATORS
confidence	feeling confident feeling able to make choices and decisions feeling motivated engaging with the idea of change
being active and able	engaging in activities and achievements deriving a sense of accomplishment having enough energy for everyday life (general good functioning) having a sense of vitality
satisfaction with life	day to day feelings (happy, relaxed, content, safe, positive; depression, anxiety, stress, anger, alienation, despair) level of satisfaction with life
feeling connected with others	being in touch with family and friends (seeing someone once a week or more) relationship with support workers opportunities to meet new people availability of support in times of need (e.g. having people you can turn to when needing a lift, needing help when ill in bed, needing to borrow money etc.) feeling part of the community

M. CONSERVATION

Impacts advance the conservation of natural and cultural heritage, natural ecosystems, and biodiversity. covers: sites of natural or historic value, biodiversity, research and education regarding conservation

CONSERVATION

FOCUS	POINT	POTENTIAL INDICATORS
conservation of natural spaces, heritage and biodiversity	conservation (restoration) of natural spaces, areas of natural beauty or special scientific interest	area of natural space (e.g. habitats, forests, water bodies, coastlines) conserved
	transformation of derelict, uninspiring and wasted spaces	area of natural space restored or created (area of derelict or brownfield sites converted)
		number of trees planted
	conservation (restoration) of sites and areas of historic interest or heritage value	number / area of heritage sites protected (restored)
	protection of wildlife, plant species	population numbers (changes) of wildlife / plant species
		number of species protected
		response from sector, special interest groups on value and effectiveness of conservation
	provision of environmental protection (from flooding, erosion, local air quality etc.)	air quality measures, diminished environmental risk
linked educational programmes and research	encourage learning	number of school visits to conserved space
	links to schools, educational facilities	number of school children visiting conserved space
	running of educational programmes and activities	number of educational programmes run (attendance)

THE GOOD ANALYST METHODOLOGY FOR IMPACT ANALYSIS AND ASSESSMENT (MIAA)

	enhance public understanding of the benefits and importance of the environment and heritage	provision and distribution of information relating to the environment and heritage (number of leaflets distributed, documents downloaded etc.)
	inform policy agenda on relevant environmental and heritage issues and enjoy political support	involvement in policy making (see **j. Information, Understanding, Expression**)
community benefits	enhance specialist knowledge	number of research documents published (sector / academic responses to research)
	use of conserved space for community purposes (e.g. events, walks, youth meetings, the arts)	number of community organisations using conserved space
		number of community events (e.g. walks, youth meetings, arts performances) taking place in conserved space (attendance)
	use of conservation area for social enterprise	number of social enterprises using conserved space
	people engage with others as they use conserved area (build social networks)	number of local people participating
		levels of volunteering
		increased social capital (see h. **Safety and Community**)
	local people are involved (invest time and energy in creating and sustaining natural / heritage spaces)	
	contribution to community health and regeneration: • time spent outdoors • health benefits • regeneration of area, sustainable development • reflection of local culture and heritage	

INVESTING FOR GOOD

N. GREENHOUSE GAS EMISSIONS

Impacts serve to reduce global greenhouse gas emissions.
covers: sustainable agriculture, energy, green building, sustainable transport

SUSTAINABLE AGRICULTURE

FOCUS	POINT	POTENTIAL INDICATORS
sustainable agriculture	organic farming	volume of organic produce
		area of land farmed sustainably
		associated reductions in greenhouse gas emissions and environmental damage (reductions in use of fertiliser, mitigation of soil erosion etc.)
	locally grown food	availability of farmer's markets
		availability of locally sourced food in shops

ENERGY

FOCUS	POINT	POTENTIAL INDICATORS
renewable energy generation	energy generation	MWh of renewable energy generated
		reduction in CO_2 emissions
		sale of Certified Emissions Reductions (CERs)
		retirement of Certified Emissions Reductions (CERs)
		lifetime greenhouse gas emissions (of project, installation, product)
energy efficiency	energy consumption	use of energy from renewable sources
		amount (proportion) of renewable energy used
	energy savings	amount of energy saved through efficiency improvements
		policies and initiatives introduced to improve energy efficiency
		related reductions in greenhouse gas emissions
research and development	new renewable energy innovations	number of publications
		number and impact of innovations developed

GREEN BUILDING

FOCUS	POINT	POTENTIAL INDICATORS
construction and renovation of buildings with an environmental purpose	construction renovation	number of units built / renovated to high environmental standards value and built area of units built / renovated to environmental standards BREEAM (or other e.g. LEED, Passivhaus) accreditation related reductions in CO_2 emissions lifetime greenhouse gas emissions (of project, building)
core environmental focus areas for green buildings	design and construction phase • monitor and reduce CO_2 emissions and energy consumption relating to site activities and transport to and from site • implement best practice with respect to air pollution (dust), water pollution • use of responsibly-sourced and environmentally-sustainable construction materials • re-use of existing building structure or facade • external hard landscaping to meet specifications of green guide • life cycle costing of building (LCC analysis) • construction waste diverted from landfill (re-used, recycled)	reductions in CO_2 emissions, pollution, consumption, waste
	health and well-being • provision of daylighting, natural ventilation, views, minimised microbial contamination	percentage of building daylit, naturally ventilated

energy • reduction of CO_2 emissions and increased energy efficiency achieved through environmentally-aware use of: • passive design strategies • insulation • building services • IT equipment • low to zero carbon technologies (photovoltaic cells, wind generation, ground source heat pumps etc.)	reduction in energy use and related CO_2 emissions
transport • consideration of transport options including public transport, cycling and pedestrian access, restricted parking facilities	increase in use of sustainable transport
water • due consideration of water consumption, water metering, leaks, water recycling	volume of water consumed, recycled
waste • provision for recycling	volume of waste produced, recycled (proportion)
land • re-use of previously developed land • awareness of the ecological value of land, mitigation of ecological impact, enhancement of site ecology and biodiversity	area of brownfield or previously contaminated land reused populations of species of plants / animals conserved

pollution	• minimise building-related pollution (substances, light, noise)	pollution levels
use	• building user guide provided to users on sustainable building management	building performance in use

SUSTAINABLE TRANSPORT

FOCUS	POINT	POTENTIAL INDICATORS
sustainable transport	provision of sustainable transport alternatives (e.g. electric vehicle, car pool) encouraging use of sustainable transport	uptake of sustainable transport alternative increase in number of people walking, cycling, using public transport reduction in levels of road congestion reduction in levels of unsustainable company travel (air miles, car miles) related reduction in CO_2 emissions

O. CONSUMPTION, WASTE, POLLUTION AND RECYCLING

Impacts safeguard natural resources and promote environmentally responsible practices
covers: consumption, waste and recycling, pollution and clean up, water

CONSUMPTION, WASTE, POLLUTION AND RECYCLING

FOCUS	POINT	POTENTIAL INDICATORS
consumption of resources	schemes to increase resource efficiency	reduction in exhaustive consumption of valuable resources
general waste and recycling	production and recycling of general waste	waste • percent recycled • percent re-used • percent donated • amount (tonnes) to landfill • change in amount of waste going to landfill (reduction)
	use of recycled materials	proportion of input materials from recycled / re-used sources
harmful waste, pollution	production and treatment of harmful waste	SO, NO, PM etc., ozone depletors toxic and chemical emissions to water, soil (reductions); volume and type hazardous waste, spills (prevention) initiatives on mitigation volume of harmful waste responsibly disposed of (remediation of environmental damage from pollution) impact on locality (measures of local pollution levels and consequences)
water	water use and efficiency	volume of water consumed volume of water recycled volume of rainwater harvested volume of water saved through efficiency schemes
	wastewater	volume of wastewater discharged to sewer or other water bodies (if applicable) impact on locality (measures of local pollution levels and consequences)

7. APPENDIX D: SAMPLE DIAGRAMS

The process of scoring produces number values, and therefore facilitates a diagrammatic presentation of results (in addition to the rating and discourse elements of the impact analysis report). The scores in the various sections can be used to make graphics showing the key features or impact profile of the organisation under analysis. Equally, repeat scorings of an organisation can be used to make graphs tracking the organisation's impact over time. Capital providers who work with a number of different organisations can plot these together on a single graph, average results, use the mapping operations as a basis by which to subdivide their portfolios into pie charts according to different criteria, and so on.

The diagrams in this appendix give two brief examples of how results can be used graphically (impact profile pentagons and impact/time graphs). Many other formats are of course possible, and can be designed to meet the requirements of whoever is using the MIAA, and what they want to show. The relevance of the methodology itself is simply that it produces a field of meaningful numerical data, which is the single prerequisite for making good diagrams.

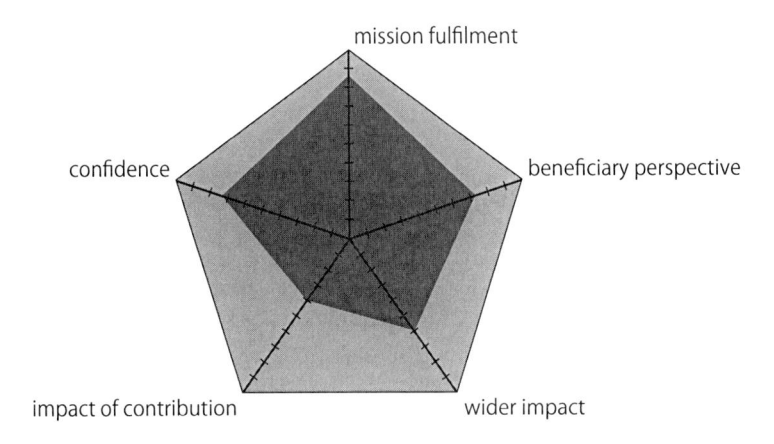

Figure 7.1 Diagram showing the key features of an investment in a social-purpose organisation. The axes represent the MIAA scores on: the three impact perspectives (Mission Fulfilment, Beneficiary Perspective, Wider Impact); the Confidence perspective (representing confidence in the financial viability of the organisation); and the Impact of Contribution (representing the impact of the investment capital on the organisation itself). The points of the inner (irregular) pentagon mark the organisation's scores (scaled proportionally) on the different measures.

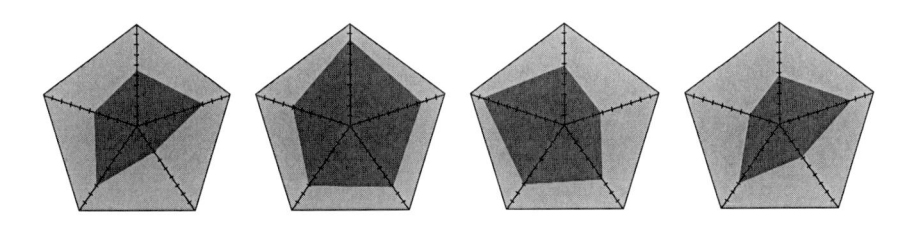

Figure 7.2 Further examples for different organisations.

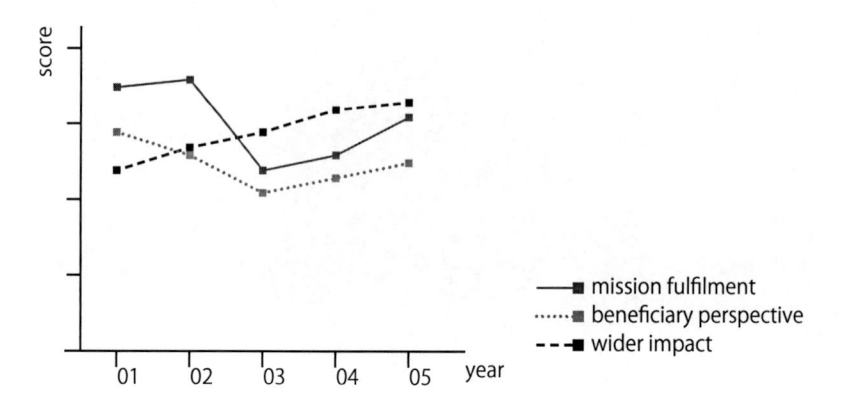

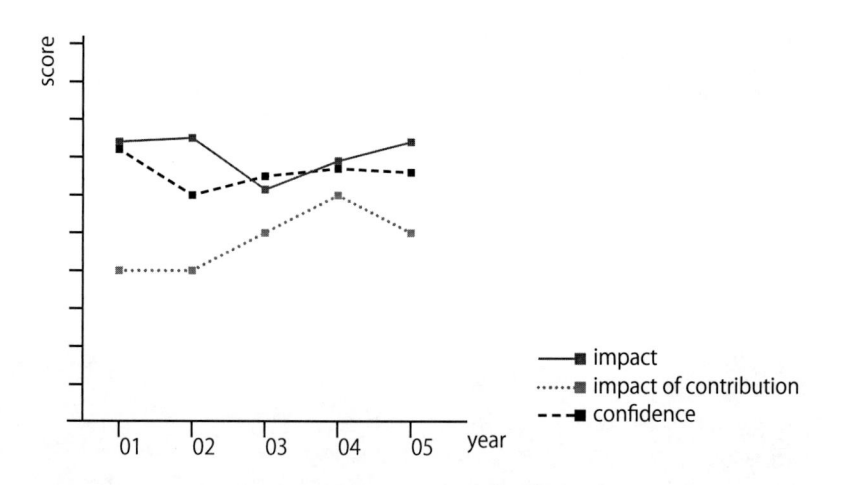

Figure 7.3 Two graphs for a single organisation over a five year period. The upper graph shows the organisation's performance on Impact with respect to the three Impact perspectives. The lower graph shows the Impact (aggregate), Impact of Contribution and Confidence over the same period (scaled proportionally to relate to one axis).

THE GOOD ANALYST METHODOLOGY FOR IMPACT ANALYSIS AND ASSESSMENT (MIAA)

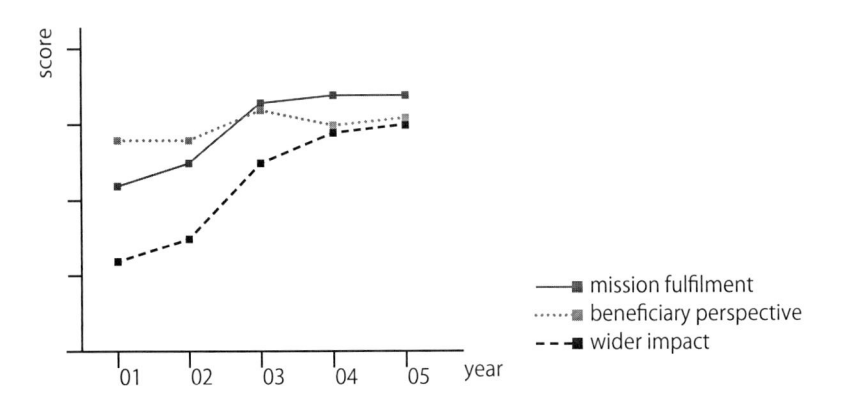

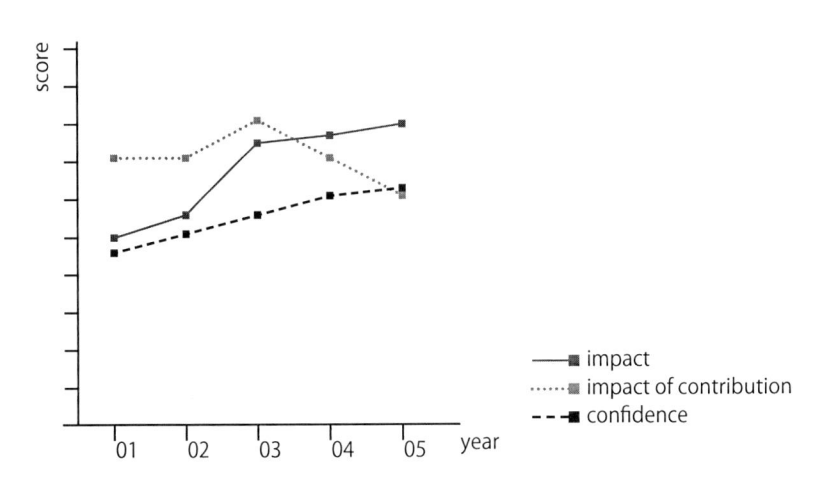

Figure 7.4 As of Figure 7.3 but for a different example organisation.

PART III
GUIDELINES FOR HOW TO MEASURE AND REPORT SOCIAL IMPACT

0. PREFATORY NOTES

Over recent years there has been a tremendous upsurge in demand for organisations — across both charitable and commercial sectors — to provide more information about their social and environmental impact. This has been driven in part by the invention of the internet, and the new thirst it has created for information. At the same time, globalisation has led to a much stronger sense of how interconnected different things and pieces of information really are, and therefore of the importance of reporting beyond the financial bottom line.

For social-purpose organisations, these developments have brought considerable opportunities, as well as some new pressures. On the one hand, the sudden interest in impact reporting promises to give organisations the opportunity to tell their story to a wide and switched-on audience. However on the other, a lack of standardised procedures has often made the practice of impact reporting seem complicated, and even daunting. Organisations that want to engage with social impact measurement have often been faced with the question of how to go about it, and how to resource it. Meanwhile, a profusion of reporting requirements from various bodies — often presented in different but confusingly overlapping terms — has allowed the real aims and advantages to become obscured.

At its core, impact measurement seeks to gather crucial information about an organisation's activities, and use it to relate the overall change achieved, over a particular period of time, to people's lives and the environment. As such it offers value on four key fronts, represented by its four primary readers.

1. You the social-purpose organisation
Most importantly, the information coming out of social impact measurement should speak to the organisation itself. The measurements you take must be geared toward the outcomes that matter to you. Knowing more about your organisation's outcomes allows you to see what works, to identify where improvements can be made, and to learn from results when making decisions about the future.

2. Your funders, investors, clients and the public
Impact measurement and the results it produces provide a powerful tool for communicating what your organisation does. Transparent reporting promotes trust and confidence among funders and investors, and allows you to talk to clients and bid for contracts with tangible evidence of your outcomes in hand. Also, in a broader context, being able to articulate your impact enables you to inform the public about your work — raising awareness not only of the issues that concern you, but also of the things that can be done.

3. Your beneficiaries and staff
The qualities of clarity and transparency can equally be of value to your beneficiaries. Where appropriate, impact measurement can help beneficiaries understand the services, processes and outcomes you offer, and to see the real benefits that accompany them. Being able to define your impact allows you to celebrate success — rewarding achievements, and inspiring new beneficiaries to engage with your organisation and start measuring their own progress. This equally can be of enormous value to staff, for whom impact measurement can be a means to see the difference they have made, and feel that their efforts are indeed bringing about the kind of change that first inspired them to do the work they do.

4. The sector
As impact measurement and reporting spreads, it allows different organisations to communicate more effectively and share results. This can form the basis for greater understanding and for drawing together effective approaches and techniques, thus driving improvements across the sector. It also equips representatives of the sector with a more complete and convincing body of information when negotiating with government over planning and policy.

How To Use These Guidelines

This document is aimed at helping social-purpose organisations that are looking to develop their own social impact measurement and reporting. It draws on a wide body of existing research to set out the fundamentals of measuring impact and working with results. It takes a non-prescriptive approach: we believe the first requirement of any impact measurement system is that it is of greatest use to you. Rather than telling you what you have to measure, the Guidelines lay down an explicit framework as to how your ideas, your activities, and the things that matter most to you can be assembled into a coherent system for impact measurement and reporting.

The Guidelines are geared toward measuring impact going into the future. While attempts to look at impact after the fact are likely to run into problems with collecting data retrospectively, and prove time-consuming and incomplete, an impact measurement system that is formulated in advance is far simpler and lighter to apply. It allows you to identify progress as it is happening, and to plan, measure, evaluate results, and improve in a thought-through and effective fashion.

You will probably be familiar with much of the material outlined below, and will have addressed a number of items already. While certain aspects are covered in some detail, it is not necessary when building your own impact measurement system to respond to every point. The idea of the Guidelines is to provide a relatively complete vocabulary of parts for impact measurement, from which you will want pick and choose to some extent. A differentiation is made between core elements, which require address, and more advanced features, which may be more or less appropriate according to your organisation's size, stage of development, and the unique aspects of your mission and approach.

The basic principles of impact measurement are that you communicate clearly what you are trying to achieve, how you are working to achieve it, and the progress you have made so far. The process of building a comprehensive picture is divided into five sections:

1. Defining Your Mission
2. Mapping Your Activities and Measuring Your Impact
3. Beneficiary Involvement
4. Using Results
5. Communication

Each section starts with a summary of action points, and then works through these in greater detail, expanding on how to understand and approach certain aspects, and on what constitutes an effective response. At the end of the final section is an outline for an impact report.

While these Guidelines are concerned primarily with how to structure your impact measurement and reporting, they are supported by an online

INVESTING FOR GOOD

Dictionary of Indicators,[1] which addresses particular sectors and impacts, and some of the indicators commonly used to measure them. As with the Guidelines, the Dictionary is not intended to be a prescriptive list, but rather serves to provide you with easy access to some of the progress that has been made in the field of impact measurement, and to furnish you with useful pointers and ideas. Together these two documents should help you build your impact measurement system on top of the work that has already been done.

---

1 See www.investingforgood.co.uk/dictionary

1. DEFINING YOUR MISSION

	ACTION POINTS
CORE	**write a mission statement** • check your mission statement for vision, clarity and relevance
	set out the context and scope of your work • identify the problem you are seeking to address, research the context, investigate broader trends, and formulate a strategy
	make sure you know your beneficiaries • identify who your beneficiaries are, ensure you understand their needs, and define the change you are trying to make

In order to start measuring your impact, it is necessary first to define what you are trying to achieve.

This section is divided into four parts:

1.1 Mission Statement
1.2 Understanding the Context
1.3 Focus, Scope and Strategy
1.4 Your Beneficiaries

1.1 Mission Statement

All organisations must have a mission statement. A mission statement defines an organisation's core aims, and what it hopes to change and achieve.

A good mission statement demonstrates the following qualities:

vision
The mission statement encapsulates the organisation's vision. It is not simply a summary of what it does nor (in the case of a charity) its legal objects. Instead it looks to the difference the organisation seeks to make, and the purpose of its activities.

clarity
The mission statement clearly establishes the organisation's area of focus and particular approach. It gives direction to the organisation as to what it does, and also what it does not do.

relevance
The mission statement is meaningful in relation to the organisation's activities, outputs and outcomes. It sets up key aspects of the organisation's work, and lays the foundations for its achievements. The organisation's impacts tangibly further its stated mission, and the mission guides and informs the medium to long term strategy.

To be effective, the mission statement should be in active use and subject to review:

in use
Staff, volunteers, and trustees are aware of the mission statement and are guided by it.

reviewed regularly
The mission statement is reviewed regularly (e.g. annually) to ensure it remains relevant and representative as the organisation develops.

1.2 Understanding the Context

While the mission and activities of an organisation may be quite specific, necessarily these take place within a wider context. Organisations seeking to address particular problems need to situate their impact within the context of those problems, and of any other actions taking place. Demonstrating you are aware of the broader picture, and that your mission addresses it meaningfully, serves to validate your approach and show that it is thought-through.

Understanding the context can be seen in relation to the following issues and questions:

identifying the problem
What is the root problem your organisation seeks to address?

researching the context
What is the scale of the problem? What are the causes? How is it impacting people's lives and the environment?

government
What is the government position on the problem? Is it taking any action on a national, regional or local level? If so, how is this affecting things?

other organisations
Are there other organisations tackling the same problem, or similar problems elsewhere? What approaches and techniques are they using? What evidence have they published about their results?

broader trends
What are the larger developments you see happening within the sector and in relation to the problem in the coming years?

1.3 Focus, Scope and Strategy

Having established your understanding of the context, it is possible to define the focus and scope of your own organisation. This marks out the field within which you will be carrying out your mission, and forms the basis for developing your strategy.

The focus and scope can be determined in relation to the same fields as above:

focusing on the problem
Which specific parts of the greater problem does your organisation focus on? Which aspects have you prioritised and why?

working within the context
What is the scope of your work, and the scale on which your activities are taking place? What is the physical area your organisation covers? What is the magnitude of the impact you are seeking to achieve in relation to the greater problem, and within the specific field where you are active?

government
How does your address of the problem relate to any government interventions or initiatives? How do you engage with local authorities and government?

other organisations
How does your organisation relate to other organisations in the sector? Do you: communicate; learn from each other (e.g. share techniques and approaches); enter into partnerships; compete?

broader trends
How does your understanding of any broader trends you see taking place inform what you are doing?

Your strategy should be guided by your mission, and responsive to the particular context laid out by your focus and scope (i.e. the strategy focuses on the identified aspects of the problem, works within the context, and takes account of government, other organisations and broader trends). While the mission communicates the high level aims, the medium to long term strategy (e.g. three to five years) sets out the specific fields of application, as well as clearly defined goals.

1.4 Your Beneficiaries

The final part of defining your mission and the framework for its application is to define your beneficiaries and the specific needs you are trying to meet. Your beneficiaries are the people whose lives you are primarily seeking to change, or the environments you are hoping to impact.

The key aspects of your beneficiaries can be captured in relation to the following points:

identify your beneficiaries
In order to reach and have an impact on your beneficiaries, it is important to set out who your beneficiaries are, and how they are defined. Features which distinguish your beneficiaries may include: a particular geographic area; a section of the public; people with specific support needs; a conservation area, species or climate change concerns; other social-purpose organisations (e.g. for umbrella

organisations). Identifying and describing who your beneficiaries are creates a target group for your impact.

research and assess the needs of your beneficiaries
Having determined who (or where) you are trying to reach, the next step is to research and identify the specific needs your beneficiaries present. This may involve consultation with beneficiaries and those around them to understand their views and priorities, or research into an area or issue. The resulting needs assessment allows you to ensure that your mission and approach responds to your beneficiaries (for more on this see 3. Beneficiary Involvement).

define the change for your beneficiaries
Here the question is: what benefits are you seeking to deliver to your beneficiaries, and what actual change are you ultimately trying to achieve? This creates the framework for understanding the progress made toward that change, and sets goals for beneficiaries to recognise and agree with.

understand the context of your beneficiaries
Understanding the context of your beneficiaries involves: considering any other needs or conditions that may affect your beneficiaries; identifying any other existing or potential resources that may be available; and recognising any other (support) organisations that may be working with your beneficiaries.

define your stakeholders beyond your primary beneficiaries
Beyond your primary beneficiaries, your organisation is likely to have impacts on a range of further stakeholders. A stakeholder is defined as anyone whose life is materially affected by an organisation and its activities, and in that sense has a stake in what it does. Prominent stakeholders often include: staff; the local community; suppliers; shareholders. Consideration of your stakeholders allows you to identify further impacts and benefits you may be achieving or could achieve. It also acts as a check upon any unintended or negative consequences.

2. MAPPING YOUR ACTIVITIES AND MEASURING YOUR IMPACT

	ACTION POINTS
CORE	**draw up a map of your activities** • make a map that is forward-facing and incorporates your plans • link your planned activities to anticipated outputs and outcomes
CORE	**choose indicators to track your outputs and outcomes** • for help selecting specific indicators see the online Dictionary of Indicators at www.investingforgood.co.uk/dictionary • set targets and objectives for the indicators you are going to track • draw up a system for collecting results
	look at your wider impacts • consider your wider impacts for things to include in your impact measurement system

Having defined your mission the next step is to turn to the business of how you actually further and fulfil it. This involves mapping your activities — i.e. the things you as a social-purpose organisation do — and identifying what you are achieving.

This section is divided into five parts:

2.1 Drawing Up an Activities Map and an Impact Chain
2.2 Your Theory of Change
2.3 Choosing What to Measure
2.4 Setting Targets and Implementation
2.5 Wider Impacts

2.1 Drawing Up an Activities Map and an Impact Chain

Drawing up a map establishes how your activities fit together, and how they link on the one side to your original mission, and on the other to the generation of positive social impact. Having a map enables you as an organisation — and your stakeholders — to see clearly and understand what you are doing.

What are you doing?
The first step is to set down the main operational activities that your organisation is concerned with. These are the things you do on a daily basis, and constitute your major operating costs (and, where applicable, your trading income). If you are pursuing operations on multiple fronts, then the breakdown of activities should show how these things relate to each other.

What are you planning?
It is important that your map is forward-facing. Having defined your mission, context and scope (see 1. Defining Your Mission), your plan is your opportunity to respond directly through your activities. Setting out your plan and mapping it is critical to developing a measurement system that can track your activities as they are taking place, and subsequently provide results that are relevant to what you are trying to achieve. Your plan must include both details of what you are actually going to do, and objectives defining what you hope to achieve.

What are your outputs and outcomes?
Your outputs are the immediate results of your operating activities (e.g. services supplied, goods distributed). These are the most tangible product of the work you do. Following from your outputs are your outcomes. These represent the actual social and environmental benefits achieved. While your outputs focus on the things you as an organisation deliver directly to your beneficiaries, your outcomes speak more of how your beneficiaries absorb these things into their own lives, and experience change. As such, it is the outcomes that show an organisation's real impact, while the activities and outputs show the mechanics of how it is brought about.

Linking these elements together forms an impact chain.

| ORGANISATION | → | ACTIVITIES | → | OUTPUTS | → | OUTCOMES |

INVESTING FOR GOOD

2.2 Your Theory of Change

Your impact chain, through linking your activities to outputs and outcomes, forms your theory of change. Essentially it puts forward a process for how your organisation achieves impact, and how it understands that impact will play out in the lives of beneficiaries and the wider environment. It identifies what you are doing, and how this will drive change.

The work of social-purpose organisations often leads to outcomes with a number of stages or layers. Interventions may impact a beneficiary's life on multiple fronts, and continue spreading and creating new impacts into the future. A single output (for example, a beneficiary entering and completing a job training programme) may have an obvious and direct outcome (the beneficiary finding a job), but this may in turn drive a wave of further benefits (enhanced confidence, improved social skills, boosted income, better quality of life, etc.).

In drawing up your organisation's impact chain, you will need to decide how far to follow your outcomes, and to what extent you can be sure they are the result of your own outputs. This will relate to the focus and scope of your mission and operations, and will likewise imply a focus and scope for your impact measurement. A good impact chain displays the following qualities:

coherent and reasonable
The links within the impact chain are coherent (i.e. one follows the next with a strong sense of cause and effect), and the outcomes claimed are reasonable in relation to the activities and outputs. In particular, the outcomes are clearly attributable to the related outputs (at least in part if not in full).

other factors are acknowledged
Where the outcomes and benefits enjoyed by beneficiaries derive from a number of sources — including the organisation's outputs and other factors — these other factors are listed and acknowledged.

supported by evidence
Where possible the theory of change implicit within the impact chain is supported by evidence or examples showing that the approach really works. These may come from research in the field, or from past results of the organisation itself.

has a clear timeframe
Some outcomes may be readily forthcoming; others may be the long term goal of many years of progress and development (where this is the case it is often useful to identify a "journey of change" with intermediary outcomes along the way — see 2.3 Choosing What to Measure below). Outcomes should be set within a clear timeframe to help establish: how the impact chain operates; when different impacts are expected to be forthcoming; and, where long term outcomes are involved, how these follow on from the initial impact.

relates to mission, context and strategy
The impact chain relates to the mission statement, context and strategy laid out earlier (see 1. Defining Your Mission). This ensures:
- outcomes further the mission: the impact chain and the outcomes it produces further the stated mission in a meaningful fashion
- the approach is informed by understanding: your understanding of the context, and your research on the particular needs of your beneficiaries, feeds into the approach described in your activities map and impact chain. The impact chain should serve to corroborate your strategy, and confirm you are addressing the issues you have identified, and that your activities constitute an effective response.

has scope
The scope of your mission and active operations should likewise be reflected in your impact chain. Equally, the impact chain defines the scope of the impacts you are claiming for your work, and thereby — as these are the impacts you need to track — provides the scope for your impact measurement system.

2.3 Choosing What to Measure

The exercise of mapping your activities and drawing out an impact chain serves to highlight the key elements in your process. The next step toward measuring your impact is to start tracking these elements — i.e. your outputs and, where possible, your outcomes. This is done using indicators.

Indicators are the specific things within an impact measurement system that you take measurements of. Straightforward indicators around outputs tend to follow direct quantities (e.g. number of goods distributed, number of people receiving services), and provide a useful tool for checking you are carrying out your activities efficiently. It is important also to capture some information as to what these numbers mean in terms of impact by looking further to your outcomes, and considering what indicators can be used there.

The selection of indicators is a highly particular task, and will be determined by an organisation's unique mission, approach, and the specifics of its impact chain. **There is no rule as to what precise indicators should be used, and it is organisations themselves who, once clear about their own activities and impact chains, are best positioned to select the indicators most suitable to them.**

The indicators you choose form the basis for your social impact measurement system, and go on to define what impacts you can report effectively upon. It is therefore critical they capture the essential information about what you are doing, and about what matters most to you. It is likely you will want to consider using several different indicators to take in both quantitative and qualitative aspects of your work. Typically these may include:

- measurements of output volumes
- measurements of change in beneficiaries' lives or behaviour (e.g. avoiding high risk activity, attending job, school etc.)
- staff reports on progress (e.g. of beneficiaries' attitudes, outlook)
- results from beneficiary questionnaires, surveys or groups

Impact measurement systems are often stronger if they can take in several perspectives. The direct experience of front-line workers may provide valuable insights into how change works for beneficiaries, and what to look for from an indicator. Input also from beneficiaries themselves can serve to ensure that the indicator is measuring impacts that are real, and are valued. At the same time, managers have to maintain perspective on what is feasible, and on what kind and scale of measurement system will suit them operationally.

It is of particular importance that indicators are capable not only of demonstrating success, but also of identifying areas where improvements can be made. The transparency implied by a meaningful use of indicators reveals both good and bad performance, allowing organisations to see what strategies work best, and to learn and respond accordingly.

In choosing your indicators it is important to check for the following qualities:

relevant — the indicators must be relevant to your goals and indicative of the real benefits outlined in your mission

responsive — the indicator must be sensitive to change (i.e. an indicator which always gives the result "3" is not useful)

time-bound — the indicator must fluctuate over time with the element being tracked, and do so within the reporting period (i.e. to provide new readings at least from one year to the next)

specific — the indicator must be specific as to what is being measured and exist on a well-defined scale, such that the measurement can be taken again in the same way (e.g. for the next reporting period) and on the same scale (e.g. a "3" will mean the same thing)

consistent — the indicator performs consistently (i.e. repeat measurements give the same result), forming a reliable basis for comparison (the primary requirement is to be able to compare results from one reporting period to the next)

practical — the indicator must be simple and relatively quick and cheap to use, making it practical and realistic for using regularly (at least once a year)

Organisations working with long term projects may not be able to measure and demonstrate final outcomes on a year-on-year basis. In such cases it is useful to consider what stages or "milestones" are passed on the way, where progress becomes visible through the achievement of intermediary outcomes (themselves in time contributing to the final outcomes). This is sometimes referred to as a "journey of change". Formulating a journey of change for your beneficiaries allows you to find indicators for specific points along that journey.

For organisations in other fields, maintaining a situation from year to year (i.e. no change) may in fact be a key outcome, and represent an important impact. Here indicators that demonstrate stability are applicable.

In either situation, as is the case generally, the purpose of impact measurement is not to produce a large number or high ratio, but to identify what — given your organisation's mission and approach — you hope to achieve over a reporting period, and then to choose indicators that can tell you whether or not this has happened.

To help you start thinking about indicators and how to understand and structure your measurement system, these Guidelines are accompanied by an online Dictionary of Indicators.[2] The Dictionary draws together a body of commonly used points of focus and indicators — some specific to particular sectors, and some more widely applicable. It is not intended to be a prescriptive list, but rather serves to provide you with easy access to some of the work that has been done in the field of impact measurement, and to furnish you with useful pointers and ideas.

Combining your impact chain with your indicators allows you to start constructing your impact measurement system.

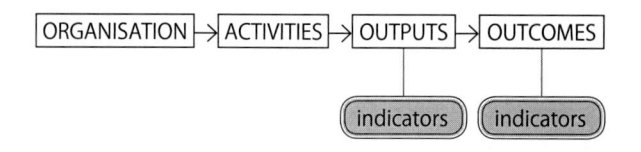

ORGANISATION → ACTIVITIES → OUTPUTS → OUTCOMES
                              | |
                          indicators indicators

Your impact chain elements, and the indicators you use to track them, will define what information you collect, and so in turn set the focus and scope for your impact reporting.

2.4 Setting Targets and Implementation

SETTING TARGETS

Indicators give you a way of tracking particular elements within your impact chain. With these laid out clearly, and with a means for measuring them, it is possible to start setting targets and specific objectives, and to relate these to the goals defined in your strategy and the core aims of your mission.

---

2 Again: www.investingforgood.co.uk/dictionary

Not all targets need to be numerical quantities (e.g. x beneficiaries receiving services, x goods distributed), but having a clear objective for your planned activities can be useful when later assessing achievements and reviewing progress. In particular, it helps answer the key questions:

- Have you carried out your plan as intended?
- Has it been successful?

For example, you may introduce a new activity with the aim of raising the confidence of your beneficiaries. Information from a pertinent indicator (e.g. from a survey question, or a particular aspect of observed beneficiary behaviour) can subsequently help you understand if this has indeed worked.

For each element in your impact chain, there should be a corresponding intended result. Outputs are commonly tracked against discrete targets, while outcomes often relate better to objectives or aims for beneficiaries.

Incorporating targets and objectives into the structure of your impact measurement system adds a further layer.

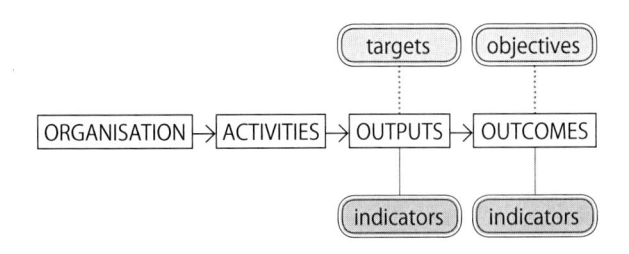

Thus by this stage:

- your plan is laid out in an activities map and impact chain
- the elements of the impact chain are tracked by indicators
- the indicators are accompanied by targets and objectives
- the targets and objectives key into your strategic goals, and thus represent a furthering of your mission and core aims

IMPLEMENTATION

With the indicators, targets and objectives in place, it is necessary to integrate them with your operations. This means that information on your indicators is collected at the appropriate time (attempts to collect information after the fact are likely to prove time-consuming and less accurate). For some indicators this may involve implementing a monitoring system to ensure levels are recorded on a regular basis (e.g. weekly, monthly). For others it may mean setting particular times to gather information (e.g. conducting a survey at the start and end of a programme). Making a plan for how you are going to collect data on your indicators is a good way to get the most out of your measurement system, and in the most efficient fashion. As this plan determines when information becomes available, it sets the timeframe for regular impact reporting.

In order to demonstrate a change has taken place, it is often useful to have a least two readings — most obviously a reading taken before and after an activity (such as a programme or service), with the difference between the two being the change achieved.

2.5 Wider Impacts

It is important that the primary focus of your impact measurement is on your primary impact — i.e. positive change for your beneficiaries. However this impact may have further implications in the wider context, which are useful to consider when evaluating your overall impact.

Impacts tend to spread outwards and multiply, becoming ever larger and more diffuse, and the total value of your wider impact will almost certainly be impossible to track. There are nevertheless sometimes tangible economic or knowledge benefits that result from the work of social-purpose organisations, and these can be a powerful compliment to the measured social benefits.

When approaching wider economic benefits, there are four common areas to consider:

> **savings in direct government expenditure**
> Do your impacts bring about a reduction in direct government expenditure — for example through beneficiaries coming off or becoming less dependent on state support?
>
> **savings in government costs**
> Do your impacts bring about a reduction in high risk behaviour and associated government costs, for example, through reduced crime

rates or reduced accident and injury rates (e.g. related to alcohol or drug abuse)?

enhanced local value
Do your impacts bring about enhanced local economic value, visible for example through new businesses moving into the area, new investment being attracted into the area, or an increase in local property values? If so, can you demonstrate tangibly how this enhanced value is attributable at least in part to your organisation's work (e.g. new businesses cite your outcomes as significant factors in the decision to open in your locality)?

economic multipliers
Does your organisation supply a boost to the local economy through the use of local suppliers, or by providing local employment or attracting visitors to the area (who then use local services)?

If wider economic benefits are relevant to your organisation's activities, then indicators relating to these can likewise be built into your impact measurement system and implemented operationally. This may involve recording specific information — for example on the change in dependence on state support among your beneficiaries, or the total amount of money you spend locally. For commonly used indicators relating to wider economic benefits, see the online Dictionary of Indicators.

As well as economic benefits, an important part of your wider impact may relate to knowledge benefits — for example, greater levels of public or government awareness, or improved understanding among organisations within the sector (for organisations engaged in advocacy or campaigning, these are likely to be among key outcomes). Knowledge benefits of this kind most commonly relate to:

levels of public awareness
Do your activities boost levels of public awareness around the issues you are seeking to address? Engagement with public awareness may include events and media exposure as well as your ongoing publicity activities.

communication within the sector
Do you engage with other sector organisations and with relevant bodies or associations? Activities may include participation in events

and conferences, research and publications, and the formation of partnerships.

involvement with policy making or local planning
Are you involved in policy making or local planning, or informing government advisory bodies? How is your knowledge of your beneficiaries and your impacts influencing the policy context or government response?

involvement with (local) business
Are you working with local or non-local businesses, informing them of your mission and how they can play a role? Are there ways in which you have changed how commercial sector companies do business?

As with other benefits, knowledge impacts can be drawn into elements and assigned appropriate indicators (again see the Dictionary of Indicators for some practical examples). If knowledge impacts constitute a significant part of your overall impact, again it may be useful to integrate them into your impact measurement system.

3. BENEFICIARY INVOLVEMENT

	ACTION POINTS
CORE	**make sure your beneficiaries know you** • consider beneficiary awareness, access and inclusion
CORE	**make sure you know your beneficiaries** • consult with your beneficiaries over their needs, views and priorities
	look to involve your beneficiaries in your work • consider beneficiary participation in planning activities and the provision of support • engage beneficiaries with how you measure impact

Beneficiary involvement is not so much a component of an impact measurement system as a principle that runs throughout it. According to the nature of your beneficiaries and your approach, different levels and kinds of beneficiary involvement will be appropriate. For organisations working with beneficiaries who are themselves less able to participate or express their views, an important route toward beneficiary involvement can be to engage with family members, carers or others who are able to contribute on their behalf.

It is essential for almost any organisation to ensure it has engaged with its beneficiaries sufficiently to be confident that:

- the needs of beneficiaries are recognised
- the effects of activities upon beneficiaries are understood
- the resulting impact is something wanted and valued by the beneficiaries themselves

Beneficiary involvement is a compelling way to help establish that an organisation works with its beneficiaries, and empowers them wherever possible to achieve their own personal goals.

Bringing beneficiary involvement into impact measurement assists organisations in expanding from a narrow focus on services (measuring volumes of services provided, activities delivered) to incorporating the beneficiary perspective (measuring benefits received, outcomes experienced). It can be an important check to help ensure that the development of beneficiaries, rather than the development of the organisation itself, remains at the heart of operations.

This section lays out some prominent aspects of beneficiary involvement that may be useful to consider when thinking about your beneficiaries and how they may become involved.

3.1 Beneficiary Awareness, Access, Inclusion and Consultation
3.2 Developing Activities with Beneficiaries
3.3 Measuring and Assessing with Beneficiaries
3.4 Supporting Beneficiaries to Become Service Providers

3.1 Beneficiary Awareness, Access, Inclusion and Consultation

Engagement with beneficiaries starts with establishing a good, representative and informed relationship.

beneficiary awareness
Are your beneficiaries aware of your organisation and the support you provide? Addressing this may include: consideration of distribution of information about your services (e.g. newsletters, website, hotline); your media presence; leveraging community resources and word of mouth networks.

beneficiary access
Can your beneficiaries access your support? Access issues may include: transport (e.g. access by public transport); disabled access requirements; financial barriers; communication (where language is a problem); paperwork (forms that need to be filled in and could prove challenging).

beneficiary inclusion
Is your outreach inclusive, representative and diverse? This involves consideration of the make-up of your target population of beneficiaries, and confirming that the actual beneficiaries you reach are appropriately representative (typically with regard to issues such as gender and ethnic minorities). Inclusion relates to awareness, access and uptake of your support (i.e. are the people aware of and accessing

your services representative?), but also to successful outcomes — i.e. does your support result in successful outcomes for your beneficiaries equally, or do certain groups do better or worse than others? If so, is there anything you can do to make your successful outcomes more inclusive?

beneficiary consultation
The aim of consultation (building on researching beneficiaries' needs) is to ensure beneficiaries' views and priorities are represented, and that the impact being achieved is in fact what beneficiaries want. Where possible, consultation seeks to engage beneficiaries in understanding the process of the impact, and for the benefits to be identified and described by the beneficiaries themselves. Activities should be recognised as suitable, appropriate and effective. Following consultation, the information gathered should support planning and development.

3.2 Developing Activities with Beneficiaries

Here the focus is on beneficiary participation, and on using the understanding and energy of beneficiaries to drive activities forward. First it is important to ensure your beneficiaries have the knowledge and skills needed to participate, and, where appropriate, to support the development of these skills (e.g. awareness of issues, confidence). Beneficiary participation in the development of your activities may include:

- beneficiaries being given choice regarding activities
- participation groups where beneficiaries are invited to contribute suggestions
- beneficiaries identifying and defining issues to be addressed
- beneficiaries being involved in designing activities
- beneficiaries leading activities

Beneficiaries — with direct experience of the issues under address, and as active service users — have a unique perspective upon your activities, and often valuable insights. Participation enables beneficiaries to share their skills, knowledge and experience with each other and with the organisation.

3.3 Measuring and Assessing with Beneficiaries

Here beneficiary participation is extended to the process of how to understand and assess impact. Key aspects are:

- participation in the definition of progress
- participation in identifying what is important to understand and observe impact, and in the selection of appropriate indicators
- participation in the design and testing of surveys / questionnaires

Beneficiary involvement on this front helps ensure that your impact measurement system captures the aspects of what you do that really bring about meaningful change in the lives of your beneficiaries. It can also assist beneficiaries in being able to see and measure their own progress, and develop confidence in change.

The follow-on from beneficiary participation in how to measure impact is then to share results with beneficiaries, and invite feedback. This helps you agree upon lessons learned, and inform your planning for the future. Feedback from beneficiaries further presents a useful opportunity for beneficiaries to review their own roles, and the engagement system as a whole.

3.4 Supporting Beneficiaries to Become Service Providers

Beneficiary involvement reaches its most complete form when beneficiaries are able to start contributing to the impact themselves, and enter into the support side. Integrating beneficiaries into support networks helps those networks capture fully the skills and understanding of beneficiaries, while enabling beneficiaries to use their experiences productively, and to give something back to the community.

Beneficiary engagement with service provision may include:

- volunteering
- employment within the support organisation

- engagement with advocacy (on behalf of other beneficiaries)
- inclusion of beneficiaries on boards
- beneficiary ownership of the support organisations (e.g. through shares, cooperatives structures)

4. USING RESULTS

	ACTION POINTS
CORE	**review your activities** • review the key events, achievements and changes that took place over the reporting period
CORE	**assemble your results** • using the information you have gathered, present your inputs, outputs and outcomes
	check your results • review the validity of your results (ensure they are objective, robust and balanced) • check for any unintended or negative outcomes • check for additionality
CORE	**review your performance** • assess your performance against your targets and objectives, and against previous years • review what went well, what went less well, and what external factors affected things • draw out the lessons learned
CORE	**plan for the future** • in light of your results and external changes, make a plan for the upcoming reporting period • review your mission and medium to long term strategy

The central purpose of assembling an impact measurement system is to produce useful results. While 2. Mapping Your Activities and Measuring Your Impact was aimed at constructing an impact measurement system facing forward into a reporting period, section 4. Using Results is concerned with using the results gathered at the end of a reporting period.

Having collected data on your indicators, the next step is to draw it together with relevant information about the period, and to evaluate your results. This allows you to develop an informed informed response, and to ensure that, going into the future, your organisation is improving, and that your activities are really having the impact both you and your beneficiaries want.

Adding these processes to the previous impact measurement system shows the structure connecting back into itself:

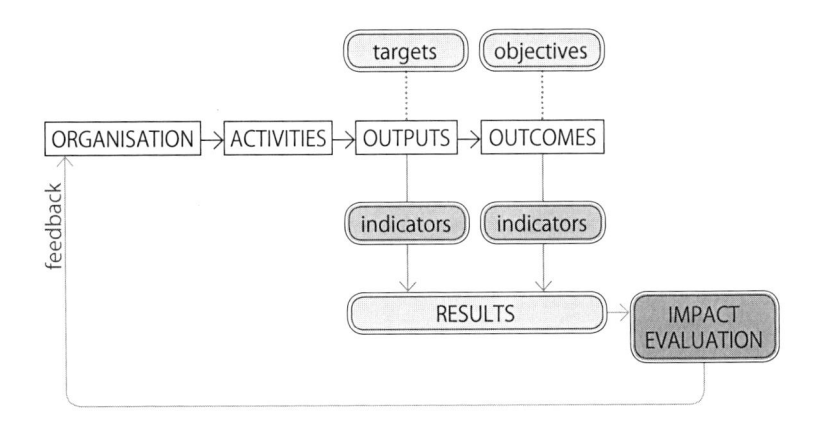

This section on using results is divided into two parts:

4.1 Treating Results
4.2 Reviewing and Responding

4.1 Treating Results

To be meaningful, your results need to be seen in the context of what you have been doing, and how you have been measuring it. The following stages set out a framework for treating your results.

REVIEW YOUR ACTIVITIES
Before presenting your results it is useful to review briefly the activities they relate to, and the reporting period over which they were taken. This involves firstly setting out the timeframe of your results, and the scope of the activities and impacts they are addressing. This essentially means revisiting your activities map and impact chain (see 2.1 Drawing up an Activities Map and an Impact Chain above), and updating it where necessary in view of what happened over the period. An activities review should cover:

- your key events and achievements over the reporting period
- any improvements introduced or new services or products offered
- any significant changes

ASSEMBLE YOUR RESULTS

The information collected on your indicators allows you to assemble your results and, with reference to your impact chain, present your impact. Here your impact measurement system furnishes you with the vital information to give an account of:

- your outputs delivered over the reporting period
- your outcomes achieved or forthcoming
- comparison of your results with the initial targets set out for the period

Alongside your outputs and outcomes, it is important also to state the costs involved. This focuses on the inputs and resources used, asking:

- what inputs were used?
- were the intended (planned) inputs forthcoming?
- what other inputs were used?
- how does this compare with previous years?

Relevant costs include the operating costs of your activities and, where applicable, the investment involved (e.g. in new facilities, project space etc.).

Where relevant, you may also want to give an account of your wider impacts (see 2.5 Wider Impacts above).

VALIDATE YOUR RESULTS

The presentation of your results should be accompanied by an outline of how you gathered your information. Just as reviewing your activities involves revisiting your activities map, validating your results involves revisiting your plan for impact measurement (see 2.4 Setting Targets and Implementation above), and sketching out a brief account of your impact measurement system as it was used. This covers things like how you collected and treated your data, and serves to ensure that your results are:

objective
Your methods for collecting data are objective, and the results produced give a reasonably complete picture (i.e. relevant data is not omitted, and results are in keeping with the realities of outcomes). Any underlying assumptions are clearly laid out and where necessary supported (these may relate to the treatment of samples or proxies, or any important background information used to build an understanding of impact or for calculations with results).

robust
The data is robust (i.e. accurate, consistent, specific etc.). You may in particular wish to check for double-counting (e.g. a beneficiary showing up multiple times using the same service), and consider what the margin of error may be in your results.

balanced
The data is able to capture both good and bad performance. This is essential to facilitate a balanced assessment, and for identifying areas for learning and improvement. While weaknesses in results may appear disappointing, organisations which demonstrably learn from their activities are far more convincing models of efficiency than those which are unaware of how well or badly they are doing.

Where resources allow, the strength of your results can be further validated through use of, and reference to, third parties. This focuses on benchmarking and external verification.

benchmarking
Information from third parties, such as comparable data and results from other organisations, and findings from relevant research, can help you build a case for what your impact is doing, and how it relates to the wider sector. Comparison with other results looks in particular to the use of benchmarks. These can serve to situate results in a meaningful context, and build a framework for understanding what different values mean. You may find benchmarks for the specific indicators you are reporting on may not be immediately forthcoming, or not applicable to your particular approach. However as impact reporting matures it is likely benchmarks will become increasingly prevalent, and information about benchmarks common to particular sectors will become more available. Where possible, by looking to other organisations working in similar fields, or to other sets of data

where there is a useful degree of comparability, you may be able to start developing your own benchmarks. Also, and perhaps more importantly, you can benchmark against your own performance. The consistent use of a valid measurement system will furnish you with comparable results on a year-on-year basis. These give you a vital understanding of the development of your own impact through time, and allow you to set benchmarks that are meaningful to you.

external verification
This may take the form of a third party auditing your results, or the results may be compiled using an accredited process, with the final report being assured in some way (i.e. "stamped" by the relevant assurance body). External auditing or accreditation can be an expensive process, and is something you will want to consider in relation to the size of your organisation, and the resources you have available.

BEYOND DIRECT RESULTS

Your impact measurement system focuses on what you do, and on measuring the anticipated positive benefits. Understanding the true net value of these benefits however requires also looking beyond your impact chain at things it is not focused on. This includes checking for unintended or negative outcomes, and addressing the question of additionality.

unintended or negative outcomes
These constitute part of an organisation's impact and should be counted among the results. Such outcomes may have been missed in planning, but have emerged over the course of operations, or they may have been anticipated (and justified on account of being less significant than the benefits). Where possible these outcomes should be measured in a manner similar to how positive outcomes are measured so the results for the two are comparable.

additionality
Additionality poses the question of whether the impact achieved is something that occurs over and above the business-as-usual scenario (sometimes also referred to as the "deadweight scenario", "the counterfactual case", or "what would have happened anyway"). This asks: if the organisation were not present and carrying out its

activities, would the same or similar outcomes nevertheless have been achieved? This may be the case if:

- beneficiaries are able to access the same or similar services or products from elsewhere
- another social or environmental purpose organisation would have stepped in to supply these services or products
- the situation would have fallen back on a government response
- the commercial sector would have responded to the situation
- beneficiaries would have been able to make progress on their own, without the services or products

Some organisations may be pioneering new fields, where the their activities are clearly additional. For others — for example those supplying services to local authorities, where the services contract would most likely have been fulfilled by someone else — the additionality may be considerably less. Where the situation would otherwise have reverted to government or the commercial sector, there may have been some impact, though most likely of a different kind to that offered by the social-purpose organisation. In the absence of any intervention, it is possible some beneficiaries would have been able to achieve positive and even similar outcomes anyway (e.g. found a job without the training offered, found housing etc.). Here it is useful to think about what proportion of beneficiaries would reasonably have achieved such outcomes without your support (you may wish to compare the outcomes of similar beneficiaries living in different areas with no support, or look to prevailing ratios).

Where significant changes would have taken place without the work of your organisation, the additionality of your impact is the impact over and above what would have happened anyway.

The aim of addressing additionality is not to reduce or recalculate your impact, but simply to show you are aware of what other options or outcomes are available to your beneficiaries. This helps you understand the nature of your impact, and tell the story of the real difference you have made. In this way, a transparent treatment of additionality can be a constructive part of evaluating your results.

INVESTING FOR GOOD

4.2 Reviewing and Responding

Reviewing and responding to results comprises the two essential tasks of assessing performance, and learning and improving.

ASSESSING PERFORMANCE
Assessing performance focuses on the progress made toward your goals for the period, and any changes that have taken place. The evaluation of results looks to:

targets, objectives and past performance
The most immediate aspect of assessing performance is to consider your results in relation to the targets and objectives you set yourself at the outset of the reporting period, and against your performance over previous reporting periods. Essentially this asks:
- were you able to meet your targets and objectives?
- is your performance improving?

It is important to investigate and explain your results, reviewing what was successful, and where there were shortcomings. It can also be useful to review your initial plan for the year, and to evaluate how effective your strategies have proven.

changes over the period
To give a full account of your results you will need to address things that emerged during the period which affected performance. This can include external factors such as changes in government programmes or policies, or other changes in the local environment or the context of your activities that have affected demand. It can also relate to internal changes in structure, funding or strategy that came through during the reporting period.

feedback on results
Your assessment should also incorporate consideration of any feedback you have had on your results, especially from beneficiaries and staff. This can give valuable insight on which activities and outcomes were most valued by your beneficiaries, and which were considered most successful by frontline workers. Feedback also offers

a perspective on the quality of your results, and feeds into a review of your impact measurement system.

review your impact measurement system
As a part of reviewing your results, it is important to review also your impact measurement system, and to address the question of whether the indicators you are using are performing as intended (see 2.3 Choosing What to Measure above), and whether your results really capture the impacts that matter most to you. The impact measurement system should also be reviewed for how practical it has proven in terms of time and resources, and how helpful it has been. The review should seek to identify any points where the system could be refined, or the implementation streamlined.

LEARNING AND IMPROVING

The power of impact measurement is that it provides your organisation with essential information about your activities from which you can learn and improve going into the future. The most important part of reviewing results is therefore to address the questions:

- what can we learn from our results and experience?
- how can we respond?

immediate lessons
The performance assessment in relation to targets and objectives for the period should yield important lessons regarding your activities, providing clear pointers for adaptations and improvements, as well as demonstrating where it is effective to keep doing more of the same.

going into the future
It is also critical to review performance in terms of progress toward longer term goals, and the fulfilment of your mission. For this it is useful to consider your performance in relation to the context of the problem as initially laid out (see 1.2 Understanding the Context above), and to ask: what has changed? This relates to your own longer term work within the context, and any trends taking place at the national or international level.

Consideration of the changing context leads to an assessment of upcoming risks and opportunities. These may include:
- changes in policy or regulations

- changes in demand or funding
- new technology

The crucial question is then how this relates to your planning and strategy for the future. Your plan should be responsive to the lessons of your results, and the new risks and opportunities identified. The plan sets out explicitly where past performance will influence activities for next year, and where adaptations are being made in relation to the changing context. As previously, the plan must tie into your activities map and impact chain (adapted to remain forward-facing), and provide clear targets and objectives for the next reporting period. Alongside these is your plan for ongoing impact measurement, which equally must remain in step with developments in your activities, outputs, and outcomes.

Building on your plan for the next year, and likewise responding to your results and context, it is important to review also your medium to long term strategy, and to establish that your mission continues to define your organisation's core aims.

5. COMMUNICATION

	ACTION POINTS
CORE	**write an impact report**
CORE	**publish and distribute your impact report**

The most obvious visible output of an impact measurement system is high quality regular impact reporting, resulting in improved transparency and communication. This communication can in fact be a meaningful part of your impact.

Impact reporting most often centres on an annual report, though results can inform more frequent newsletters and other pieces of published research. You may wish to combine your social or environmental reporting with your annual company report and financial accounts, or create a separate impact report.

Adding the report to the previous diagram completes the overall impact reporting structure:

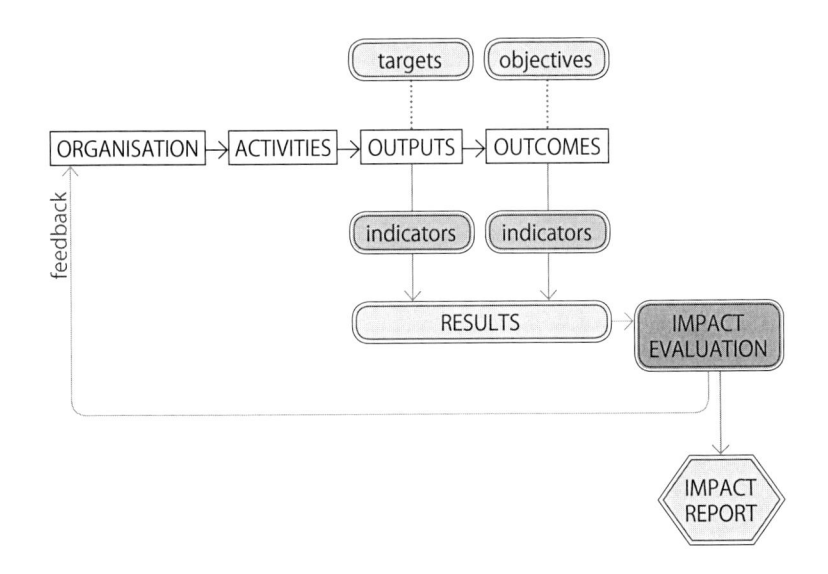

INVESTING FOR GOOD

These Guidelines have been primarily concerned with assembling an impact measurement system, and using it to gather information, learn and improve. The work involved in this process however feeds directly into impact reporting, which is primarily a reflection of the structure producing it — i.e. an account of your activities, results, and consequent plans for the future.

This section provides an outline for an impact report, detailing the core points to be included, as well as further points for expansion according to what is relevant to your organisation, and how detailed you want your report to be. The points are derived from the action points of the previous sections, which fit directly in. In this way, impact reporting should be less a burden than a natural extension of your impact measuring and reviewing processes.

This section is divided into two parts:

> 5.1 Qualities of an Impact Report
> 5.2 Outline for an Impact Report

5.1 Qualities of an Impact Report

The most important qualities for an impact report are that it is clear, readily available, and appropriately distributed.

Clarity is about ensuring that your impact report can be easily understood by the general reader, as well as by relevant professionals. Your impact report is your way to communicate the work you do and the impact you have made, and to be of greatest value should be comprehensible to the widest possible audience. This may involve unpacking any specialist terms and, where you have used very specific indicators, explaining what these results mean. You may also wish to outline briefly any important aspects of the sector that a general reader might not know.

Making your report available means telling people you have published an impact report, and telling them where they can get a hold of a copy. The most obvious channel for this is likely to be your website, where the report should be available to download via a clear, quick and simple link, probably not more than a few clicks from your homepage. In addition to this you may wish to make printed copies available (e.g. at your activities centres or service points).

Beyond general availability, there are a number of particular audiences for your impact report, and it is important to check they are being reached by your distribution. These include:

funders and investors
Your impact report allows your supporters to see and feel the positive benefits their money has helped generate.

relevant planners, policy makers and government bodies
Your impact report can provide important insights into the problem you are tackling and how your response works. These can inform and shape the government's position and any response it may have.

other sector organisations
Sharing results with other sector organisations facilitates: the comparison of approaches and techniques; moving toward the establishment of benchmarks; and the promotion of common understanding and good practice. Your impact report can be an important contribution to communication on this front.

your beneficiaries
For your beneficiaries, your results can be a powerful way to see and understand your process, and to engage with change. Results can serve to inspire beneficiaries as well as celebrate success. If your general impact report is not readily comprehensible to your beneficiaries, you may wish to consider creating a separate version that presents the key information in an appropriate form.

5.2 Outline for an Impact Report

	REPORT ELEMENT	refer to
	Summary	
CORE	date of report and period covered	–
	overview of report	–
	Mission	
CORE	What is your mission?	1.1
	How do you understand the problem you are seeking to address?	1.2
CORE	What is your response in terms of your key aims, approach, and the basic direction of your work?	1.3
	How are you responding to your beneficiaries?	1.4, 3
	Activities and Results	
CORE	What were your activities over the reporting period? • can you map your activities?	2.1
CORE	How does these translate into your impact? • can you outline your impact chain?	2.2
CORE	What were your results for the reporting period? • what indicators did you use? • what values were recorded (outputs, outcomes)? • what inputs were used (costs, resources)?	4.1 2.3, 4.1 4.1 4.1
	What were your wider impacts?	2.5
	Were there any unintended or negative outcomes?	4.1
	How do you address the question of additionality?	4.1
	Reviewing and Responding	
CORE	How do your results compare with your targets and objectives for the period? What were the key factors?	2.4, 4.2
CORE	What are the lessons learned, and what changes are you going to make as a result?	4.2
	How do you see the external situation developing (opportunities, risks)?	1.2, 4.2
CORE	What is your plan for next year?	4.2
CORE	How do you intend to measure its success (targets, objectives)?	2.4, 4.2
	What is your longer term strategy for the future?	1.3, 4.2

GLOSSARY

activities the work a social-purpose organisation engages in to further or fulfil its mission. The most prominent activities typically are the organisation's front-line services (e.g. services or products supplied to beneficiaries), which are supported by the organisation's internal operations (e.g. procedures, accounting, management issues etc.).

additionality the impact of a social-purpose organisation that stands over and above any change that would have taken place had the organisation not been active. Changes that would have taken place anyway are referred to as part of the business-as-usual or BAU scenario (see below). The difference between the situation with the organisation's impact and the BAU scenario reveals the organisation's additionality.

beneficiaries the people, communities, areas and aspects of the natural world which a social-purpose organisation seeks to reach through its activities, and who stand to benefit as a result.

business-as-usual scenario (BAU scenario) what would have taken place or happened anyway among the beneficiaries and in the context in which a social-purpose organisation is active were the organisation not to be active. This is a hypothetical or alternative scenario that considers what outcomes are likely to occur in the absence of the organisation. The BAU scenario, sometimes referred to elsewhere as "the deadweight scenario", "the counterfactual case", or "what would have happened anyway", is evoked by the question of additionality (see above).

capital providers parties who supply capital to social-purpose organisations, either in the form of donated capital, or as a loan or investment, or as a purchase of services on behalf of beneficiaries. Capital providers as a group includes funders, impact investors, donors, grant-makers, commissioners of social services (e.g. local authorities), philanthropists, venture philanthropists, socially-motivated funds, foundations, lenders to the social sector, and so on.

company a standard for-profit company (as opposed to a social-purpose organisation).

contribution the capital injected into a social-purpose organisation by a capital provider, and which thereby fuels the organisation's activities.

impact the positive social or environmental change achieved by a social-purpose organisation.

impact chain a representation of how an organisation achieves its impact by linking the organisation to its activities, and the activities to outputs and outcomes.

impact investment an investment in the social sector. Impact investments are driven by impact, and define themselves more by the impacts they achieve than by their attractiveness on a straight risk-return financial basis. They are nevertheless financial products (as opposed to donations). Capital is invested in on the grounds that the principle will be returned, usually with the expectation of some degree of financial return. Impact investments structures include debt products, equity investments and loans.

impact investors socially or environmentally-motivated individuals, funds or institutions that invest in impact investments.

indicators specific variables measured by organisations in order to track their outputs and outcomes. Indicators may relate to direct quantities (e.g. number of hours of training provided) or to qualitative aspects of an organisation's work (e.g. levels of beneficiary satisfaction), but to act as an indicator, the organisation must have a means to measure the indicator's value.

inputs the resources a social-purpose organisation draws on in carrying out its operations and activities. These include financial resources (e.g. investment capital, funding and donations, revenues) as well as human resources and, potentially, materials or space made available, support from other organisations, services or advice given in kind, etc..

outcomes the social or environmental benefits following from outputs (as produced by an organisation's activities). Outcomes relate to the positive change experienced by beneficiaries as outputs are absorbed into their lives and the impact takes effect.

outputs the products or services a social-purpose organisation is immediately involved in the delivery of, and which issue directly from its activities (e.g. services supplied, items produced). Outputs do not in and of themselves represent the impact, but lead to outcomes.

social-purpose organisation an organisation whose primary aim is the achievement of social or environmental impact (social and social-purpose are used throughout this book to include both social and environmental aims). Social-purpose organisations include charities, or non-profit organisations, and social enterprises (which may be registered as Community Interest Companies or as limited companies). Social-purpose organisations are sometimes referred to as mission-driven organisations, and primacy of mission is a good litmus test as to whether or not an organisation is genuinely social-purpose. In this book "social-purpose organisation" is often abbreviated to "organisation" (and as such is distinguished from "company").

social-purpose universe used to encompass the social sector and all the parties and individuals active within and around it, including social-purpose organisations, capital providers (including government), beneficiaries, employees and volunteers, policy makers, advisers and regulators, consultants and academics, and the wider body of stakeholders.

social return an awareness of the social impact an organisation is achieving that is fed back to a capital provider in return for having initially put capital in. While the social return has no financial value, the knowledge it gives the socially-motivated provider that their capital is actively and effectively driving impact can act as a form of compensation. Social returns may also be prospective: an impact investment may propose itself to investors on the grounds that it offers a high social return (while presenting a comparatively low financial return).

stakeholders any party that is materially affected by an organisation's activities. Most prominent among stakeholders are the direct or target beneficiaries, though stakeholders as a group also include the organisation's staff and volunteers, its shareholders and investees, it suppliers and purchasers up and down the business chain, and most likely the families and those close to the beneficiaries.

INVESTING FOR GOOD

FURTHER RESOURCES

Much has been written on the subject of impact. The following list provides links to some prominent organisations who have researched and published work on impact measurement, reporting and evaluation, or who are active in the field.

The Carbon Trust
www.carbontrust.co.uk

The Carbon Disclosure Project
www.cdproject.net

The Charity Commission
www.charity-commission.gov.uk

Charities Evaluation Services
www.ces-vol.org.uk

Global Impact Investing Network (GIIN) and Global Impact Investing Ratings System (GIIRS)
www.thegiin.org, www.giirs.org
see also the GIIN's Impact Reporting and Investment Standards (IRIS)
www.iris.thegiin.org

Global Reporting Initiative (GRI)
www.globalreporting.org

New Economics Foundation (nef)
www.neweconomics.org
see also nef's Prove and Improve toolkit
www.proveandimprove.org

New Philanthropy Capital
www.philanthropycapital.org

Social Impact Analysts Association
www.siaassociation.org

The Social Return on Investment (SROI) Network
www.thesroinetwork.org

The Urban Institute
www.urban.org

Tools and Resources for Assessing Social Impact (TRASI)
www.trasi.foundationcenter.org

Triangle Consulting
www.triangleconsulting.co.uk
see also Triangle Consulting's Outcomes Star
www.outcomesstar.org.uk

INVESTING FOR GOOD

The methodology presented in this book was developed with Investing for Good in collaboration with Geoff Burnand and Caroline Mason.

Special thanks to Will Murray for essential contributions regarding the use of a human rights approach in evaluating impact.

Thanks to Jeremy Mercer, Gabrielle Blumberg and Hannah Marcus for comments, insights and advice on the manuscript.

The Good Analyst ebook is available free of charge from the Investing for Good website.

www.investingforgood.co.uk/thegoodanalyst

ahornsby@investingforgood.co.uk
gburnand@investingforgood.co.uk

2012 Investing for Good

INVESTING FOR GOOD